OCOMOTION PAPERS NUMBER

BRANCH LINES TO RAMSEY

by

John Rhodes

THE OAKWOOD PRESS

ISBN 0 85361 323 0

Printed by Bocardo Press, Cowley, Oxford

Published by
The OAKWOOD PRESS
P.O.Box 122, Headington, Oxford.

BRANCH LINES TO RAMSEY

Contents

Looking from the buffer stops at Ramsey East in 1952. The cattle dock is in the foreground with the goods shed in the middle background. The signal box and engine shed had been demolished when this photograph was taken.

L&GRP, Courtesy David and Charles

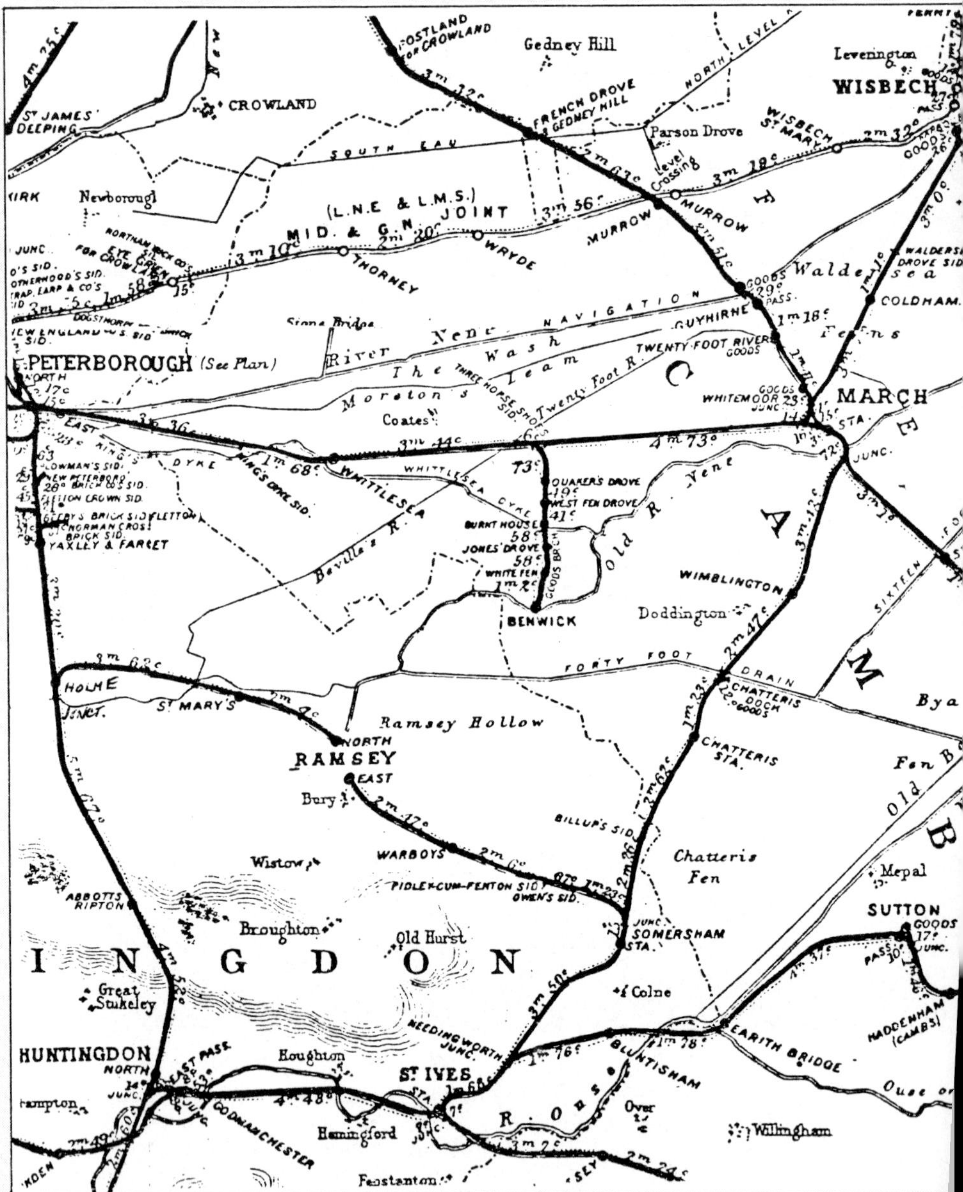

1920 Airey's Railway Map of the Area.

Chapter 1

Construction and Opening: Holme to Ramsey Section

Long before the railways arrived in the area, the Fens were, for most of the year, simply large expanses of marsh and water, broken occasionally by islands of slightly higher ground strung together by a tenuous line of trackways which were liable to disappear under the winter floods. In the eighth century the biographer of St Guthlac of Crowland had described the area north of Cambridge as a "countryside of marsh and bog and black pools of water, and winding streams, and wooded islands". The early settlers on these outcrops gave to their communities names which reflected the isolated aspect of much of their lives, tacking onto the end of the placenames variants of the old English word "ey", meaning an island; hence Thorney, Ely, Manea, Whittlesey and Ramsey itself. There is evidence that the Romans made some attempts to improve the drainage of the area, and there were later sporadic and largely unsuccessful schemes to alleviate the problem of flooding from the thirteenth century onwards. But it was not until the work of the Dutch engineer Cornelius Vermuyden in the middle of the seventeenth century that some real progress was made: sinuous and meandering river courses were straightened or by-passed by new cuts, and estuaries were widened and deepened, so that large areas of Fen country were able to be reclaimed. The respite was temporary, however; in time the new river banks were eroded, eventually collapsed, and once again thousands of acres regularly disappeared beneath flood water. By 1724, when Daniel Defoe made his *Tour through the whole Island of Great Britain*, he described the Fen country as "almost all covered with water like a sea: . . . these Fenns being as may be very properly said, the sink of no less than thirteen Counties . . . they are often overflowed."

It was not until the establishment of wind-powered pumping mills, and, later, steam-driven pumping engines, that the floodwaters began to be pushed back and channelled to the sea through their proper courses. By the mid nineteenth century Whittlesey Mere, the last of the great natural lakes (which, according to season, covered between 1700 and 3000 acres) was drained, uncovering in the process the skulls of a wild boar and a wolf, and some of the silver once belonging to Ramsey Abbey, and the Fens were at last rescued from their damp and soggy existence.

By this time, of course, railways had begun to spread throughout the country, and although the Fens provided level terrain, for the

315.—RAMSEY.

Incorporated by 24 and 25 Vic., cap. 194 (22nd July, 1861), to construct a line from Holme, on the Great Northern, to Ramsey, Huntingdonshire. Length, 5 miles 51 chains. Capital, 30,000*l*. in 10*l*. shares, and 10,000*l*. on loan. Opened in July, 1863. Worked by the Great Northern for seven years from that date.

Meetings in February or March, and in August or September, in Ramsey or in London.

No. of Directors—3; quorum, 2. *Qualification*, 500*l*.

DIRECTORS:

Chairman—EDWARD FELLOWES, Esq., M.P., 3, Belgrave Square, S.W.

W. Staffurth, Esq.

OFFICERS.—Sec., Thomas James, Solicitor, Ramsey, Huntingdonshire; Solicitor, F. W. Thorp, St. Ives, Hunts.

Offices—Ramsey, Huntingdonshire.

A copy of the Bradshaw's Shareholders Guide of 1870 showing the Directors.

most part favourable for laying tracks, engineers had already encountered some of the unforeseen problems caused by the peculiar consistency of the area's soil. As the GN main line approached Peterborough from the south in the late 1840s, it reached the edge of Whittlesey Mere, still undrained, and still sufficiently boggy to be extremely unstable: as the contractor Thomas Brassey said, if you stamped your foot a whole acre quivered. With the help of an engineer working on drainage in the Bedford Middle Level, Stephen Ballard, a plan was devised to make a platform of faggots, place a layer of peat on top, add another platform of faggots and another layer of peat and so on until the whole lot sank to the bottom of the mere, squeezing out the water and providing a solid foundation for the line of the railway.

Further complications were caused by the effect of water loss on the peat soil of the Fens. Draining the area had produced immense advantages in that the resulting reclaimed acres of agricultural land were some of the richest in the country, dark and fertile. William Cobbet had described the area in 1830 as "covered with beautiful grass, with sheep lying upon it as fat as hogs stretched out sleeping" – but in consistency the whole area was rather like a giant sponge: as the water was drained off and the soil dried out, its peaty qualities caused it to shrink, sometimes to an alarming degree. A graphic illustration of this shrinkage was provided by the experiment of the Holme Fen Post, a long metal post sunk to its full length into the ground in 1851 to the east of Holme village; a century later the soil had shrunk so much that 12 feet of the post was exposed above ground. The GN main line between Holme and Yaxley, although at one time level with the surrounding land, is now on an embankment since the soil round about has contracted and shrinkage continues to cause problems.In the drought-stricken summer of 1976 a 20 m.p.h. speed restriction had to be imposed over the 9 miles of line between Whittlesey and March because of undulations in the track caused by the contraction of the peat subsoil.

In spite of the engineering problems involved, by the middle of the nineteenth century this area of the Fens to the south and east of Peterborough had been bounded by four railway routes. These were three GE lines, Peterborough to March and Ely, and Huntingdon to St Ives, both in 1847, and St Ives to March in 1848; and the GN main line between Huntingdon and Peterborough, opened in 1850. With the main boundaries drawn, the time was now ripe for development within this rough rectangle of land, 150 square miles in area, at the centre of which was the small market town of Ramsey.

Ramsey was an old-established settlement, and for centuries had led a quiet existence in the middle of the flat Fen landscape, sheltered from the worst of the winter floods by its position on an elevated outcrop. But now, in the mid-nineteenth century, the age of Victorian expansion and invention, it began to feel the truth of what *The Times* had said earlier in the Railway Age: "To be destitute of a railway is the present-day reproach to the locality."

The earliest proposal for a line of railway serving Ramsey directly seems to have arisen as an off-shoot of the Wisbech, St Ives and Cambridge Junction Railway, opened on 1st February, 1848 under the aegis of the Eastern Counties Railway. While this route was still under construction, in 1846, Plans and Sections were deposited for an "Eastern Counties Extension Railway", branching off near Somersham and running for 6 miles 5 furlongs and 9 chains to a site in Ramsey on the south side of the main road. Robert Stephenson and M.A. Borthwick were joint engineers, but the scheme encountered stiff opposition from local landowners and was rejected in the 1847 Session of Parliament.

It was another twelve years before renewed attempts were made to link Ramsey with what was, by then, the rapidly growing and developing railway network of the surrounding area. The Cambridge, St Ives and Wisbech route was now well-established; the GN main line had been operating since 1850; and other improvements, such as the Middle Level drainage scheme, had been carried out to produce some of the most fertile land in the country. Ramsey,

ANNO VICESIMO QUARTO & VICESIMO QUINTO

VICTORIÆ REGINÆ.

Cap. cxciv.

An Act to authorize the Construction of a Railway from *Holme* to *Ramsey* in the County of *Huntingdon.* [22d *July* 1861.]

WHEREAS the Construction of a Railway from the *Holme* Station of the *Great Northern* Railway to *Ramsey* in the County of *Huntingdon* would be of local and public Advantage: And whereas Plans and Sections of the Railway, showing the Line and Levels thereof, with a Book of Reference to the Plans, containing the Names of the Owners, Lessees, and Occupiers of the Lands through which the said Railway will pass, have been deposited with the Clerk of the Peace for the County of *Huntingdon:* And whereas the Persons herein named, with others, are willing at their own Expense to carry the said Undertaking into execution, but they cannot do so without the Authority of Parliament: May it therefore please Your Majesty that it may be enacted; and be it enacted by the Queen's most Excellent Majesty, by and with the Advice and Consent of the Lords Spiritual and Temporal, and Commons, in this present Parliament assembled, and by the Authority of the same, as follows:

1. "The Companies Clauses Consolidation Act, 1845," "The Lands Clauses Consolidation Act, 1845," "The Lands Clauses Consolidation Acts 8 & 9 Vict. cc. 16., 18., & 20., and

[*Local.*]

with a population of 6,000, now found itself at the centre of a rich agricultural area, but isolated from places like Holme or Somersham except by roads which became impassable in winter. In November 1859, therefore, a proposal was put forward for a railway route which, once again, left the EC line north of Somersham station and ran to Ramsey, but instead of terminating there continued through to Holme on the GN main line, a distance of just over 13 miles. This was the first of a number of schemes, recurrent in the following years, which attempted to link the GN and EC/GE routes, using Ramsey as a focal point, none of which ever came to fruition. Optimism ran high, however, in these initial stages, and it was confidently forecast that the proposed line would carry a thriving passenger traffic, serving an area with a combined population of about 14,000 people, and that substantial goods traffic could be found in corn, potatoes, coal, iron, timber, bricks, and artificial manures. A rail route, it was said, would provide much better communication than the existing Fen waterways, whose routes were often circuitous and whose services were rather slow.

The proposals made good progress through Parliament, and by the beginning of April 1860 the Somersham–Holme Railway Bill had been placed on the list of unopposed Bills, a petition lodged against it earlier by the Middle Level Drainage Commissioners for sureties for protection of navigation having been withdrawn on 27th March. Outwardly, all seemed set for success, but beneath the surface optimism considerable difficulties were arising concerning the funding of the scheme. The estimates for construction of the line were £60,000, plus another £15,000 for purchase of land and legal expenses. The contractors, Simpson and Walker, had £25,000 worth of shares, and other subscribed capital amounted to £20,000. Borrowing powers would allow access to another £26,600, but this left a deficit of £3,400, and there was concern that this money might not be raised. On 5th May a meeting was held in Ramsey "for the purpose of determining what course to adopt in reference to the Bill now before Parliament". In the chair was the local M.P., Edward Fellowes, who was to play a major part in Ramsey's railway future, and whose influence at this meeting was sufficient to counteract the optimistic belief of some shareholders that the project was still viable. By a majority vote, the Somersham–Holme scheme was abandoned because of a lack of financial support.

The set-back was, however, only temporary. By the end of 1860 it was being reported in the local press that a new scheme was under consideration, this time rather more modest in its ambitions, a branch line 5 miles 58 chains long, running from Holme only as far as

THE GREAT NORTHERN RAILWAY COMPANY

AND

THE RAMSEY RAILWAY COMPANY

Agreement for working the Traffic of the Ramsey Railway by the Great Northern Railway Company.

AN AGREEMENT made the 1st day of July, 1862, between the GREAT NORTHERN RAILWAY COMPANY (hereinafter called the Great Northern Company) of the one part, and the RAMSEY RAILWAY COMPANY (hereinafter called the Ramsey Company) of the other part. WHEREAS the Ramsey Company was incorporated by the Ramsey Railway Act 1861, for the purpose of making a railway to commence by a junction with the main line of the Great Northern Railway, at or near the Holme station of that railway, in the parish of Holme, in the county of Huntingdon, and to terminate in the parish of Ramsey, in a field near the gas works, also in the said county of Huntingdon. And whereas the said Ramsey Company are about to complete the said railway, together with the necessary stations at Ramsey and St. Mary's respectively. And whereas the Great Northern Company have agreed with the Ramsey Company to work the traffic of the said Ramsey Railway when and so soon as the same shall be completed and fit to be opened for public traffic, and for the term of seven years next thereafter; and for the purpose of carrying out the agreement the said two Companies have agreed to enter into this contract. Now these presents witness that each of the said two Companies, parties hereto, do hereby for themselves, their successors and assigns, covenant and declare with, and to the other of them, their successors and assigns, in manner and to the effect following:—

1. That the said Ramsey Company shall complete their railway, and the junction with the Great Northern Railway at Holme, together with the necessary junction signals, station signals, stations, gate lodges, residences for gatekeepers at such level crossings as may be necessary, and all such sidings as are now agreed to by the Great Northern Company

Ramsey, where it would terminate "a few yards from the gasworks". The project had the backing of the Great Northern Railway Company, which, the newspaper writer felt, would make the proposal "more likely to succeed . . . and would be quite as advantageous to the town as the abandoned line that was to connect us with Somersham".

The proposed railway could boast that it had as Engineer a member of the aristocracy, Sir Charles Fox, who had in fact trained as a surgeon before joining the Liverpool and Manchester Railway, where he worked as a fireman and began to learn all about the technical side of railways until he was able to set up in the contracting business himself. He had been knighted for his work in erecting the Crystal Palace in 1851 and later removing it to its new site in Sydenham. In addition, a number of local worthies allied themselves to the Holme–Ramsey scheme, becoming Directors of the new Company: these included Arthur Ballantine, J. Boulter, and Thomas Darlow, the latter of whom had been largely instrumental in getting the town provided with a gas supply in recent years, and who had just presented Ramsey with a new water pump, at a cost of £15, to be used in case of fire. (The covering over of the river which used to run through Ramsey's main street had stopped the "insufferable odour" during summer that contributed to much illness in the town, but had made water difficult to obtain for the local fire brigade; hence the pump.) Edward Fellowes, having withdrawn support for the previous Somersham–Holme railway, kept aloof from this new scheme for a while, prompting some acrimonious comment in the local press about his apparent lack of interest in the wishes of his constituents for a railway. But by the end of May he had apparently decided that he ought to back the proposals, particularly in view of the fact that the scheme had by then gone unopposed through the Committee stage in Parliament, and there was little doubt this time that the necessary capital would be subscribed. To great local satisfaction, the Royal Assent was given to the Bill on Monday 22nd July, 1861. The Company, flushed with success, then announced that construction work would start immediately and that Sir Charles Fox had been instructed to survey an extension of the line from Ramsey, via Warboys, to St Ives, once again endeavouring to form a cross-country link between GN and EC routes.

The first ordinary general meeting of the shareholders, held at the Mechanics Institute, Ramsey, at 3 pm on Wednesday, 25th September was an occasion for some modest celebrations. The solicitor to the Company, Frederick Thorp, reported to his audience that there was evidence of much local support, financial and moral, for the line; in addition, "the terms upon which the Great Northern Company are

Holme Station in the early years of the twentieth century with the station staff posed for the photographer. This view, looking towards Peterborough, shows nicely the station architecture and painting livery. *Lens of Sutton*

A good view of the station buildings at St Mary's in April 1957. *D. Thompson*

prepared to work the line have been arranged, and are similar to those existing between other main and branch lines in various parts of the kingdom. The Directors cannot close their report without expressing confidence in the soundness of this undertaking, and their full belief that it will prove a great boon to the district, and of a remunerative character to the shareholders." Such optimism about the line's revenue, a familiar theme in the early years of many a railway line throughout the country, had a habit all too often of proving misplaced, but for the moment, in these euphoric days of 1861, all was unalloyed cheer. In this climate Edward Fellowes M.P. reinforced his recently-expressed support for the line in an enthusiastic speech, being promptly rewarded by an appointment to the Board of Directors, together with Arthur Ballantine and William Stafforth. William Orris and Edward Beecheno were made Company auditors at a salary of five guineas a year, and at a later meeting the composition of the Board was completed by the appointment of Thomas James, a Ramsey solicitor, as Secretary, at a sum "not exceeding £100 for the first year".

By the time of the second shareholders' meeting, on 11th March, 1862, Edward Fellowes had been entrusted with the chairmanship, and he was able to report that the capital so far subscribed amounted to £7,090, with Parliamentary and other expenses necessary for obtaining the Act standing at the very precise sum of £1,114 4*s.* 10*d.* Arrangements were being made to obtain the necessary land for building purposes, and it was confidently expected that the line would be open for traffic within the next year. The Engineer's report was equally encouraging: sites for the stations at Ramsey and St Mary's had been found, and arrangements for making the junction with the GN main line had been agreed with the parent Company.

Railway construction, however, was notorious for consuming unexpected amounts of money, and by May the Board discovered that it would need to raise another £10,000 in order to complete its projected line. Edward Fellowes, now rapidly coming to the fore as an enthusiastic and committed supporter of the line, subscribed half of this amount, and at a meeting on 12th May, even though it was poorly attended because of recent heavy rain and subsequent flooding, another £2,600 was promised from various sources. Construction was therefore authorised without further delay, under the main contractor, Mr Simpson of Ely, and the first sod of earth was ceremonially turned by the Hon. Mrs Fellowes at the beginning of June 1862. This being agricultural country, many local workers who might have been employed on the line were involved with the harvest at this time, but after this had been safely gathered in the work-force

An old postcard view of St Mary's Station showing the signal box, level crossing and old grounded coach body in the fore-

grew rapidly, and purposeful progress was soon being made. Although the branch line had to be floated across the peat soil on a base of brushwood, sand and hardcore, as had been necessary for the nearby GN main line at this point, on such flat terrain there were no major earthworks or bridges. This meant that costs could be kept reasonably low (estimates for building the line had been put at £25,512 10s.) and that work could go ahead relatively easily. But although construction could thus proceed apace, it did not do so entirely without incident. One of the workmen, Henry Dawson of Ramsey, had both his feet crushed by the wheels of a wagon which he attempted to board while it was on the move, a common practice among local men who often hitched a free ride in this way back to the town after their day's work. A similar, but much more serious, incident occurred while another of the workers, together with his wife and two children, was dropping off the horse-drawn train of wagons as it stopped at School Farm Drove. The man's 7-year old daughter Rebecca slipped as she was getting out of the truck, and fell onto the track; by this time the horses had got the train on the move again, and, even though they were pulled up as soon as the alarm was raised, the girl was run over and killed.

Meanwhile, the proposed extension of the line through to St Ives, mentioned earlier, was making progress through Parliament, and by February 1863 had passed its second reading in the Commons. At the same time, however, opposition, in the form of a rival proposal, had begun to show itself. By 1860 the Eastern Counties Railway, through a combination of energetic route-building and takeovers of existing lines, had established a virtual monopoly of the railway business in eastern England. The Company's first Secretary, John Clinton Robertson, had stated quite bluntly and immodestly that, in his opinion, the EC's influence was so great in this area that "it leaves not a single opening for any rival line". For a time, this seemed to be true: no rival company had so far managed to penetrate any further into EC territory than the boundary marked by the GN's newly-opened main line through Huntingdon and Peterborough to the north. Now, however, the GN-backed Holme-Ramsey branch had thrust an exploratory finger into this exclusive area of operations, and the threat to enlarge the scale of this intrusion by pushing a line through to St Ives was enough to stir into action the EC (which by this time had been amalgamated with various other lines to form the Great Eastern). The 1863 Parliamentary session accordingly found itself presented with a proposal for a six and three-quarter mile branch line from Chatteris, on the existing March–St Ives line, to Ramsey, a direct challenge to the Holme and Ramsey Extension Bill. As things

Class C2, No. 256, seen here passing Holme on the down main line in 1923. The Ramsey Branch line is to the left of the picture.
L&GRP, Courtesy David and Charles

Looking towards Holme from the buffer stops at Ramsey North Station in 1952. The goods shed had a unique double canopy which housed a 1ton crane whilst a further 5ton crane stood in the yard. In the background is the coal road. *L&GRP, Courtesy David and Charles*

turned out, both schemes were to be disappointed; the Ramsey Extension proposal was withdrawn at the Committee stage, apparently in the face of obstacles (largely financial) which would have made a continuation very difficult, and the GE Bill was rejected by Parliament in the same session.

March 1863 was the date on which the first optimistic reports to shareholders had suggested the line would be completed and opened for operations, but this was not to be; there were regular reports that construction was indeed "progressing very favourably" (by the end of April, for example, the intermediate station at St Mary's, a "convenient and commodious timber-built structure", had been completed by a local contractor, Mr Isaac Bateman) but the opening date slipped gradually backwards, with 1st June, mid-June, and then the beginning of July being mentioned in succession, each time with earnest professions of actually achieving a result.

Construction was not the only aspect of the railway that was not going as smoothly as had been hoped. Costs had once again begun to escalate, and the half-yearly general meeting on 30th April ("very thinly attended") was told that, in spite of all calls having been made on shareholders, there was still a debt of £1,209. Over half the estimated capital had been used, and a further £10,000 would have to be borrowed. The Engineer's report was rather more encouraging: track (ballasted with ashes rather than granite to give a lighter base over the peat subsoil) had been laid from Ramsey to within half a mile of Holme station; all culverts and bridges were complete and level crossings and fencing were in place. The engine-shed, goods shed, weighbridge and coal wharf at Ramsey station had been erected, and St Mary's station was virtually finished.

As the beginning of July arrived and still no announcement of opening had been made, the local newspaper began to get restless, and addressed the Directors in a stern editorial:

> Rumours of the proposed opening of the railway have been extensively current during the last few days and much disappointment has been felt by the Ramsey people on account of their not being permitted to avail themselves of the completed line to have attended the Peterborough Choral Festival and the Hunts Flower Show held last week. We trust the inauguration of so important an epoch in our local history will be celebrated in a manner befitting the occasion.

A last-minute hitch in the agreement between the GN and the Ramsey Railway Company delayed matters still further, which meant, as several "much annoyed" shareholders complained, that valuable summer traffic was being lost, and interest on borrowed capital was growing with no revenue to offset it. Embarrassed perhaps at the increasing public criticism, the contractor, Mr Simpson, attempted to pour oil on troubled waters by arranging, at his own expense, for a special train to Peterborough Fair on 10th July, which returned to Ramsey in the evening crowded with excited children who had been allowed to ride free of charge; they at least were reported to be "highly delighted with their visit".

At long last, an advertisement dated 18th July appeared in newspapers and on hoardings under the heading of the GNR, which had agreed to work the line for its first seven years, that the branch would open for public traffic on Wednesday, 22nd July, 1863. On the appointed day about a hundred people assembled at Ramsey's new station to see the departure of the first train, which carried 30 passengers the few miles to Holme. The carriages were decorated with a few sprigs of evergreen, while the engine was "tastefully and more profusely adorned with similar ornamentation, interspersed with flowers". A flag bearing a loyal motto was raised as the train left, but the spectators were rather sullenly silent, not even raising a cheer; perhaps they were making their annoyance felt at having had to wait so long to see the line in operation.

The opening day coincided, perhaps purposely, with the opening day of Ramsey's annual cattle fair, usually an occasion for three days of entertainment and jollification as well as the serious business of cattle trading. This year, however, the lack of enthusiasm that was apparent at the railway station seems to have affected even this highlight of the local calendar, and the *Peterborough Advertiser* reported gloomily that there were fewer stalls than on previous occasions (and these were of a "decidedly inferior character") and none of the usual sideshows exhibiting fat ladies or talking sheep. The most impressive features were apparently a Punch and Judy show and a cork model of Lincoln Cathedral made by a farm worker. Nevertheless, in spite of its inauspicious beginnings, the line was now open for business, and settled down to its daily service of six passenger trains.

At the first shareholders' meeting to be held after the opening (on 22nd September, 1863) the Directors maintained an optimistic front, even if the euphoria of a couple of years ago, when high dividends had been forecast, had now been replaced by a more cautious approach to the question of profits: the Chairman reported that he had high hopes of the line developing "a fair amount of traffic", which, if it would not pay a "high rate of interest", would still yield a "fair rate". There were still debts of £437 owing, but it was expected that these would be paid off within a few weeks. Some improvements to the line were suggested: local farmers had complained about the lack of a goods shed at St Mary's; and it was also felt that the traffic in corn was not as great as it would be if there were tramway links between stations and rivers, since an appreciable amount of grain was still brought in from surrounding farm-land by barge.

In spite of the optimism about paying off outstanding bills, money was still owing to the contractors six months later, at the next half-yearly meeting. It was also reported that traffic had still not been fully developed, and although it was stated that this was "only to be expected after so short a time of operation" it was becoming clear that ownership of the line was proving to be much more of a burden than had been anticipated; indeed, this was confirmed by an announcement from the Directors that overtures had already been made to the Great Eastern for purchase of the line, to be taken over by them after the expiration of the 7-year lease to the Great Northern. This change of allegiance from one Company to another (and a rival one at that) was apparently the result of the strained relationship which had developed with the GN over the terms for working the Ramsey branch.

The chance for a better deal for the branch which alliance with the GE presumably offered was therefore pursued with some vigour, and by the end of April 1864 the arrangements for the sale had been completed, with the shareholders to be paid off nearly at par. The Ramsey Railway Company received £36,000 and the knowledge that its future was now much more stable under the ownership, rather than the leasehold, of a well-established and powerful Company. The GE itself, having thus successfully ousted the rival GN from the extreme western edge of its territory, now turned its attention to consolidating its advantage by developing the area to the south-east of Ramsey.

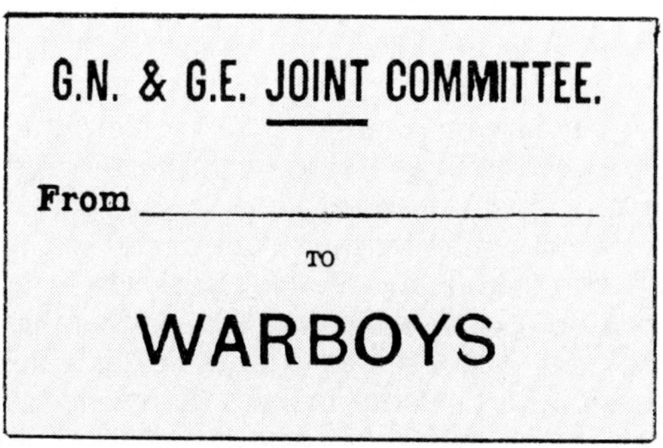
G.N. & G.E. JOINT COMMITTEE.

From ______________________

TO

WARBOYS

Chapter 2

Construction and Opening: Somersham to Ramsey Section

As part of the 1864 sale agreement with the Ramsey Railway Company, the GE had undertaken, on purchase of the line, to extend the branch south-eastwards towards Somersham, thus reviving the project of a GN-GE cross-country link. The GE had, in fact, attempted to gain access to Ramsey, and to form such a link, the previous year, 1863, when in November, plans were deposited for a nine and a half mile railway from St Ives (thus picking up the idea which, as described in the previous chapter, the Holme and Ramsey Company had had to abandon a few months earlier because of lack of money), which would make a junction with the existing Ramsey branch just west of Ramsey station. These proposals foundered on their journey through Parliament, however, and were eventually rejected. By this time, the GE had concluded its agreement for the purchase of the Ramsey line, and it reconsidered plans for an extension, eventually putting forward, in November 1864, a scheme which was a throw-back to the earliest 1847 proposals, a through link joining the GE line at Somersham.

The total length of the new line, which was authorised on 2nd June, 1865, was 7 miles, 7 furlongs, 8 chains, and it was surveyed by Charles R. Chaffins, with Robert Sinclair as Engineer. It was to run from a point "25 chains or thereabout westwards of the mile post marked 77 miles" on the St Ives and March line, leaving that line by a curve of 2 furlongs 25 chains radius, and terminate by a junction with the Ramsey Railway" at a point 12 chains or thereabouts north of the School Ground Drove, where the same is crossed on the west by the said railway".

It would appear that these extension proposals were simply a safeguard on the part of the GE to protect itself from any further attempt by the GN to encroach on its territory in this area, since, having secured permission to build the extension, the GE showed no inclination to proceed with construction. This apparent renegeing on a promise already given aroused some strong local feeling, and a sharp legal battle, taken as far as a Parliamentary Committee stage, developed between the GE and the Holme and Ramsey Directors, led by Edward Fellowes. The outcome was favourable to the larger Company in that it was deemed under no obligation to built the proposed extension, but a compromise was reached whereby the GE undertook that, if ever the Holme and Ramsey Company wanted to promote its own extension to Somersham, it would contribute capital to the sum of £30,000 to the project. There was a condition attached to

The footbridge at Somersham Station (looking north) in this early view of the busy station. Note the style of the crossing gates and lamps on the footbridge.
C. Grimwood

Just 4 miles and 31 chains from Somersham was Warboys Station and its crossing loops, seen here in 1952. On the left is the brickworks with its private sidings and, on the right, the goods shed and yard. This view is looking towards Ramsey East with the original station master's house prominently situated on the right. *L&GRP, Courtesy David and Charles*

this agreement which stated that the Holme and Ramsey Company would have to act on these proposals within 3 years, but this it failed to do, obviously through lack of money.

By the early 1870s the GE had decided that simple ownership of the Holme-Ramsey branch was not enough, and took steps to guarantee its security by applying to Parliament to have the line vested in the parent Company, which would mean that it could not be bought or taken over by any other Company without a further recourse to Parliament. The GN, seeing its last chance of any interest in the route disappearing, strenuously opposed the application, and once again the inter-Company border war was resolved by a compromise: any opposition to the vesting process was to be withdrawn in return for the GE agreeing to lease the line to the GN for 21 years. Accordingly, on 21st July, 1875, the GN, for the second time, became responsible for working the branch, on a payment to the GE of 2% per annum, such dividend to increase at a rate of a quarter per cent until a maximum of three and a quarter per cent was reached.

Although the GE had apparently abandoned the idea of a Somersham-Ramsey branch, the desire for such a link was still strong among the villagers of the area south of Ramsey, and among some prominent people in Ramsey itself. A local syndicate was therefore formed to promote a private company, the Ramsey and Somersham Railway Company, which would build the line on its own initiative and with its own money. The Company Director was Alfred Fuller of Ramsey, and the syndicate also included George Burt J.P., and J.J. Freeman, who took out at least £45,000 worth of shares and was thus a major contributor to the success of the scheme. No shares were offered to the public. George Hopkins, of London, was appointed Engineer, and the main contractors were Mowlem & Co., also of London.

At this point, the GE came back into the picture, keen to obtain an interest in the new branch, and willing, as it had been earlier, to contribute £30,000 to the cost of construction. An agreement was drawn up with the syndicate but before it could be put into execution, it was interrupted by the negotiations between the GN and the GE which resulted in the formation on 3rd July, 1879 of a joint company to share control of a number of existing and newly-proposed railway lines. (The Ramsey–Somersham line was itself to be incorporated in this joint agreement from 1st January, 1897, although the GE would continue to work it for 30% of the profits, the balance to be divided between the two owning companies.) The GE, now with more important matters to consider, again lost interest in the new Ramsey branch, and the syndicate found itself faced with the prospect of

Ramsey East Station in a derelict state on 24th July, 1955. This view illustrates the style of station building; note the grounded box van on the platform.
E.H. Sawford

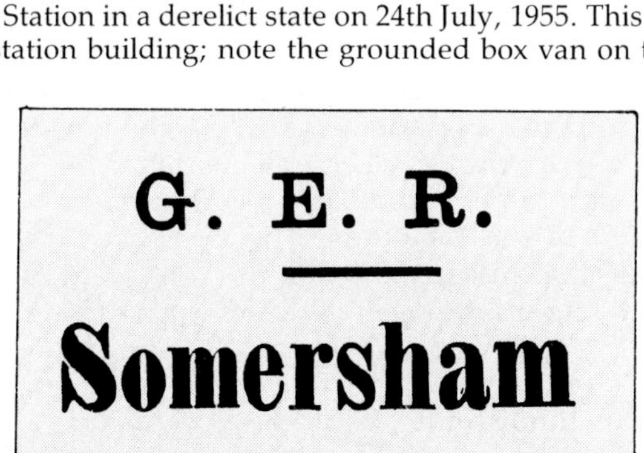

G. E. R.

Somersham

pushing the scheme through unaided. Undeterred, however, it went ahead energetically, buoyed up by the undoubted support of the local community, in particular the farmers, who realised the benefits the new line would bring. The route ran through 50,000 acres of some of the finest agricultural land in the country, a potential source of traffic so far undeveloped because of the lack of reliable or fast communications. Access to a rail link would open up a much wider market for local produce (the important market town of St Ives, for example, would be within easy reach), and land prices could be expected to rise dramatically. Six months after the opening of the Holme–Ramsey Railway, land around St Mary's had doubled in value.

Some of this land was, of course, needed for the building of the route itself, and construction eventually swallowed up 86 acres in total; although some of this cost as much as £240 per acre, much of it was able to be bought at purely agricultural prices. Further economies were made possible by the discovery near Somersham of a large seam of gravel, which conveniently provided ballast for the whole line, saving an estimated £1,200. The engineering work was generally of a light nature, with the only heavy work around Warboys, where it was necessary to excavate cuttings; the track was single throughout, although with room for double track if required at a later date, and there were only three bridges on the whole route. Stations were built at Ramsey, on the Bury Road, where a station master's house was provided as well as a goods shed, weighbridge, and granaries; at Puttock Drove (later called Warboys), whose facilities included loading banks, storage sheds, and a small house for the station master; and a goods siding was laid down at Pidley, midway between Warboys and Somersham. The branch was seven miles long and cost £65,607 12*s.* 5*d.* (land £13,086 5*s.* 3*d.*; construction £45,000; Parliamentary expenses £6,000; interest on loans £1,493 5*s.* 8*d.*; and other "general expenses" £33 7*s.* 3*d.*).

By August of 1888 the line had been completed, and on 20th September it was formally inspected by Major Marindin R.E., of the Board of Trade, without whose authority no traffic could be carried. The Major found some slight defects in the signalling of the line, and was not satisfied with the arrangements made for the working of the branch; permission to begin operations was therefore withheld pending rectification of these matters. The work would appear not to have been as easy as anticipated, since months went by without any opening date being announced. By mid-April 1889 a rumour was current naming 1st May as a likely day for the beginning of operations, but as this date came and went without any result it began to look as if the new branch line would be as capricious about opening

The station staff and a few passengers in a fine posed picture at Ramsey East in 1910. *Author's Collection*

as was the Holme–Ramsey line over a quarter of a century earlier. As before, the local newspaper faithfully pursued the elusive opening date through its columns: on 4th May it reported that "in about another fortnight we may see carriages laden with passengers steam out of the new station premises", but this forecast, too, proved false. On Saturday, 25th May there was great excitement when an engine and three carriages actually arrived at Ramsey, and word quickly spread that the line had, in fact, opened unannounced. In reality, the train was simply one of a series of engineer's inspection trains (the local paper, by this time becoming impatient, acidly commented that it hoped that this would be the final one of the series).

Part of the reason for the delay would appear to be the GE's re-entry into the line's affairs. Having built the railway, and having achieved its object, the local syndicate was apparently happy to pass over the responsibility for working it to a larger company. At the half-yearly meeting of the GE on 30th July details of the agreement reached with the Ramsey and Somersham Railway were approved and confirmed, the Ramsey and Somersham shareholders having already approved them at a meeting in London the previous day. The line was to be leased to the GE for five years from 1st July, 1889, and the Ramsey and Somersham Company was to have running powers into St Ives, the main market centre for the area. If the traffic on the line exceeded £10 per week per mile, the GE was to retain 60% of the receipts; if less than £10 it would take 65%: this arrangement, it was expected, would pay a 4% dividend for the line's owners. With agreement reached, the long-delayed opening actually seemed to be about to take place. "The much talked about and greatly anticipated local event is (we are credibly informed) fixed to take place on Monday, September 2", reported the *Peterborough Advertiser*. But once again their reliable source proved totally unreliable; modification work was still going on at the connection of the branch with the main line at Somersham Junction (a process that workmen had apparently been engaged on in a leisurely manner since June). At the beginning of September, however, there was a rush of activity: 60 men were drafted in to complete the work, and the long-awaited day of opening actually arrived on Monday, 16th September, when service trains began to operate from the new station.

Eighty-four passengers were booked on the first train to Somersham, the 8.10 am, (headed probably by engine No. 382, which had worked into Ramsey the previous day), whose progress was watched by a hundred or so local spectators. But celebrations seem to have been as muted as they were when the Holme branch was opened: the only signs of rejoicing the local newspaper reporter could find was a solitary handkerchief being waved! At Warboys there seems to have been more lively interest shown, and the platform was filled with villagers, among them some of the oldest inhabitants who had been brought in by farm cart for the event, and who sat open-mouthed as the very first train many of them had ever seen drew up in the station. The next train, a market-day special to St Ives, carried 60 more people, and at the end of the day, according to Mr Perry, Ramsey's "energetic and obliging" station master, who had been promoted there from Earith Bridge, 246 tickets had been issued from Ramsey and 130 from the intermediate station at Warboys. Watching over this satisfactory state of affairs was a varied group of dignitaries, including Mr Norton, the District Superintendent of the Great Eastern; Mr Roper, the District Goods Manager; Mr Platt, the District Locomotive Superintendent; Mr Winbolt, the District Engineer; and several members of the owning syndicate, no doubt very pleased to see such an auspicious start to the life of their long-awaited railway.

Chapter 3

Operations and Traffic 1863–1923

The inaugural service of six passenger trains a day on the Holme–Ramsey branch had been reduced to five within just over two years of the line's opening: the August 1865 timetable shows trains arriving at Ramsey at 8.40, 10.05 am, 2.05, 4.15 and 7.45 pm, having taken about 20 minutes for the six-mile journey, very sedate progress indeed. Some of these trains were carefully timed to connect with main-line services at Holme, but on some services there were awkwardly long waits necessary before the branch train set off: passengers leaving Peterborough on the 12.50 pm up train, for example, had three-quarters of an hour to kill at Holme before the Ramsey train left at 1.45.

The regular services were, however, supplemented almost immediately by a series of special excursion trains to a variety of venues. The first of these ran on Monday 27th July, only five days after the opening, when the combined Sunday Schools of the Ramsey area travelled the few miles to Peterborough. In spite of the modest scope of the excursion, the train was well loaded, with over 300 children and 50 adults, and this time, the local press reported with approval, when the train left Ramsey at 12.45 pm it was, contrary to the opening day, "amidst the liveliest demonstrations of interest on the part of the general public". The train made leisurely progress, taking an hour to reach Peterborough, where the children were assembled at the Recreation Ground to consume "a bountiful supply of buns". Games of cricket and football, a tour of the cathedral, and further buns at the Wentworth Rooms followed, the party leaving the city by the 6.30 pm train. There was a lengthy delay at Holme while they waited for the connection to Ramsey, and this prolonged the homeward journey to ninety minutes, the arrival at the home station being at 8.00 pm.

Other excursions run in the first month of operation included a cheap day trip to London (return fare 3/6) for the Odd Fellows Fête at Crystal Palace, which attracted over 100 travellers from Ramsey; a similar visit to the Palace, this time for the Foresters Fête at a slightly more expensive fare of 4/-; and a local excursion to Peterborough, when 250 people were conveyed to the city's Brass Band Concert. The branch line was now bringing Peterborough within easy reach of Ramsey folk, and many of them regularly made the journey to the nearby city. Such events as the annual October Fair were eagerly supported, and the 1863 Fair was the occasion for a cheap-day excursion train from Ramsey which was so overcrowded (420 people from Ramsey and over 100 from St Mary's) that some passengers,

HOLME and RAMSEY.—Great Northern.

Holme ......dep	8 0	9 30	1040	1 15	2 25	Sats	4 32	6 20	7 20	....
St. Mary's	Sig.	Sig.	Sig.	Sig.	Sig.	Sats	Sig.	Sig.	Sig.	....
Ramsey ....arr	8 20	9 45	1055	1 30	2 40	Sats	4 47	6 35	7 35	....

Ramsey ....dep	7 15	9 10	9 55	1240	2 0	Sats	3 30	5 55	6 55	....
St. Mary's	Sig.	Sig.	Sig.	Sig.	Sig.	Sats	Sig.	Sig.	Sig.	....
Holme 159,156a	7 35	9 25	1010	1255	2 15	Sats	3 45	6 10	7 10	....

Passenger Timetable for August 1887

RAMSEY AND HOLME BRANCH—NO SUNDAY TRAINS.

SINGLE LINE. TRAIN STAFF STATIONS:—HOLME AND RAMSEY.

from Holme.	DOWN.	1	2	3	4	5	6	7	8	9	10	11	12						
		Gds.	Mxd.	Pass.	Pass.	Mxd.	Pass.	Lgt. engn.	Pass.	Lgt. engn.	Pass.	Gds.	Pass.						
		C					Sats. only.	B	A										
		a.m.	a.m.	a.m.	a.m.	p.m.	p.m.	p.m.	p.m.	p.m.	p.m.	p.m.	p.m.						
...	HOLME... dep.	5 58	7 43	9 28	10 37	1 14	2 26	...	4 30	5 37	6 35	7 46	8 34	...	...	...	...	...	...
3½	St. Mary's arr.	6 10	...	...		...	...	...	...	...	...	...	...	...	.	...	...	...	...
	St. Mary's dep.	6 22	7 54	9 38	10 46	1 25	2 35	3 30	4 39	...	6 44	...	8 43	...	..	...	...	...	...
5½	RAMSEY...arr.	6 30	7 59	9 41	10 51	1 30	2 40	3 35	4 44	5 50	6 49	8 0	8 48	...	.	...	...	...	...

from Ramsey.	UP.	1	2	3	5	6	7	8	9	10	11	13	14	15					
		Mxd.	Pass.	Pass.	Pass.	Pass.	Lgt. engn.	Pass.	Goods	Pass.	Gds.	Pass.	Lgt. Eng.	Gds.					
						Sats. only.	B						D	E					
		a.m.	a.m.	a.m.	p.m.	p.m.	p.m.	p.m.	p.m.	p.m.	p.m.	p.m.	p.m.	p.m.					
	RAMSEY..dep	7 5	9 10	9 45	12 40	2 5	2 55	3 40	4 50	5 55	7 0	8 10	9 0	9 0	...	...	...	...	...
2	St. Mary's arr.	...	...	...	...	...	3 0	...	4 56	...	7 6	...	...	9 6	...	.	...	...	...
	St. Mary's dep.	7 12	9 15	9 50	12 45	2 10		3 45	5 15	6 0	7 26	8 15	...	9 20	.	...	...	...	...
5½	HOLME ... arr.	7 24	9 24	9 58	12 54	2 19	...	3 54	5 27	6 9	7 30	8 24	9 15	9 32	...	.	...	...	...

A May take cattle if wagons are fitted with brake pipes. See special instructions.
B To shunt St. Mary's yard when necessary.
C From New England, see train 81, page 51.
D To New England, see train 512, page 30. Will not run when 15 is running.
E When necessary. Will not run when 14 is running. To New England, see train 542, page 30.

Working Timetable for 1896

unable to find room in the carriages, had to ride in open trucks.

Freight traffic also began to establish its pattern in this opening period, and in August a local coal-merchant, John Jenkins of Huntingdon, was advertising supplies of coal available through his agent, the splendidly-named Negus Meace of Ramsey, from the stations at Ramsey and St Mary's. Prices ranged from Durham coal at 17/6 a ton to Darlington Soft at 13/-. Apart from coal for domestic use, fuel was also brought in in large quantities for the Ramsey Gasworks, already in existence before the railway arrived, but conveniently situated next to the station. As might have been expected, agricultural produce and livestock supplied the bulk of the freight traffic outwards, with consignments going to local markets such as Peterborough, or even further afield. Associated agricultural products, such as fertilizers, also formed a significant part of freight train loading, boosted by the opening in 1866 of an artificial manure works in Ramsey by Evison & Armitage (by 1888 the annual output was 2,000 tons, plus 1,000 tons of sulphuric acid as a by-product). By September 1864, after a year or so of operations, the Directors of the line were encouraged by the way the railway had captured goods traffic, and were able to report that such traffic had shown a considerable increase over the last quarter.

On such a small branch line, with generally only one train moving at a time, operations usually went without incident, but there were odd occasions when things would go wrong. It will be remembered from Chapter 1 that the underlying soil of the Holme area was peat, always liable to be unstable, and particularly so during prolonged dry weather, when the soil loses all its moisture and shrinks. The weeks of August 1864 provided one of these very dry spells, and the consequent shrinkage of the subsoil caused subsidence of the railway track near St Mary's where on 22nd August the engine of the 6.20 pm ex-Ramsey train was derailed with, fortunately, no injuries to anyone and only a minimal delay in the running of services. A more exciting incident occurred a year later, in July 1865, and concerned the daily goods train which left Peterborough at 2.30 pm, and to which, as had become usual, were attached three or four passenger coaches for the conveyance of local travellers to Holme and Ramsey. Just after it had left Peterborough it was struck forcibly in the rear by a driverless light engine, which had been left unattended in Peterborough yard with the regulator still slightly open and in forward gear; steam pressure had built up and the engine had taken off, literally under its own steam, accelerating rapidly until its progress was checked by collision with the local "mixed". The last carriage of this latter was badly damaged, and about 40 or 50 passengers received minor injuries. Reports of the incident did not mention the reaction of the driver of the light engine when he discovered that his locomotive had escaped; official retribution was, presumably, stern and swift.

It is often said that the coming of a railway to a country area very quickly took away all trade from the local carriers (who would have built up a network of horse-drawn services to all villages in the surrounding district) thereby forcing them into retirement or alternative employment. This seems to be a simplification of what actually happened, and certainly in the case of Ramsey, local carriers continued to ply their trade alongside that of the railway until well after the turn of the century, although their numbers did show a gradual decrease. Before any railway arrived in Ramsey, there was a thriving general carriage business operating regularly to places like Chatteris and Huntingdon (which was served by two different carriers on

Saturdays and one in mid-week); St Ives, with two services on Mondays; and Whittlesey, to which Henry Lant ran his cart on Mondays, Wednesdays and Fridays, leaving from the Jolly Sailor pub in Ramsey. Even well into the 1880s, when the Holme–Ramsey line had been running for over 20 years, the only appreciable alteration in the carriers' services was the fact that they had been reduced along the westward route to Huntingdon, Peterborough and Whittlesey (all of which could be reached by rail), but they were still strong in the other direction, as yet without a rail link, where three different carriers traded to St Ives.

When the Somersham line was established there was a sudden demise of competing horse-drawn traffic, and the 1890 directory of local services shows only one carrier left, operating to Huntingdon on Saturdays and to St Ives on Mondays. Some of these carriers had, however, clearly decided that the future lay not in competing with the railway but in serving it, and by the end of the century a local advertisement stated that an omnibus from the Temperance Hotel, Ramsey, would meet all trains from both stations. This was, incidentally, a service that was still in operation in the late 1920s when it was being run by a Mr Miller, a bowler-hatted old gentleman who drove an ancient Victorian coach pulled by an equally ancient horse. Driven to distraction by the local boys who used to pinch free rides by hanging on the back of his equipage, and whose combined weight was sufficient to bring the whole antediluvian contraption to a creaking standstill, Mr Miller eventually solved the problem by festooning the back axle with coils of barbed wire! In the end, his inter-station coach service collapsed through lack of patronage, and he was reduced to conveying inanimate traffic, in the form of parcels, on a hand-barrow.

Mail was another commodity which was affected by the improved communications. Back in the 1850s letters arrived in Ramsey by mail cart from Huntingdon at 7.30 am daily and were similarly despatched at 6 pm. This in itself was not a bad service as far as frequency went, but obviously it could take some days to deliver mail if any great distance was involved. The arrival of the railway speeded up the process somewhat, and also provided the town with the use of an electric telegraph for the collection and despatch of telegrams; in this way, Ramsey could at last feel in vital contact with the rest of the country.

The special excursions mentioned earlier had in general operated on a modest scale, with London as a favourite target, but in the latter years of the century visits to the seaside became more fashionable, and coastal resorts sprang into prominence to cater for this new trade.

SOMERSHAM AND RAMSEY RAILWAY.—*Single Line.*

The Trains on this Single Line are worked by Train Staff and Train Staff Ticket, according to the " Train Staff Regulations " contained in the " Appendix " to this Working Time Book. No Engine or Train is to be run on this Branch without a Train Staff or Train Staff Ticket. The Train Staff Stations are Somersham, Warboys, and Ramsey.

Miles from Somersham.	DOWN TRAINS. Week Days.		1	2	3	4	5	6	7	8	9	10	11	12
			A Gds.	B Pass.	Pass.	Pass.	Pass.	Pass.	Gds.	Pass.	Pass.	B Pass.		
			a.m.	a.m.	a.m.	a.m.	p.m.	p.m.	p.m.	p.m.	p.m.	p.m.		
	St. Ives	dep.	...	...	...	...	...	...	2 20	...	...	...	...	...
—	**Somersham**	arr.	...	...	...	...	...	...	2 35	...	...	...	...	...
	(G. N. and G. E. Joint)	dep.	7 15	9 17	10 42	11 41	12 36	2 25	2 50	3 55	5 55	7 33	...	...
2¼	Pidley-cum-Fenton Siding	,,	...	...	...	...	...	...	*	...	...	...	...	...
4¼	**Warboys**	arr.	7 27	9 26	10 51	11 50	12 45	2 34	3 15	4 4	6 4	7 42	...	...
		dep.	7 40	9 27	10 52	11 51	12 46	2 35	3 30	4 5	6 5	7 43	...	...
7	**Ramsey** (High Street)	arr.	7 50	9 33	10 58	11 57	12 52	2 41	3 40	4 11	6 11	7 49	...	...
					Mons only									

Miles from Ramsey.	UP TRAINS. Week Days.		1	2	3	4	5	6	7	8	9	10	11	12
			C Gds.	Pass.	Gds.	Pass.	Pass.	Pass.	Pass.	Pass.	Gds.	Pass.	D Pass.	
			a.m.	a.m.	a.m.	a.m.	a.m.	p.m.	p.m.	p.m.	p.m.	p.m.	p.m.	
—	**Ramsey** (High Street)	dep.	5 45	8 10	8 20	10 5	11 5	12 4	1 51	3 18	4 30	5 20	6 54	...
2¼	Warboys	arr.	*	8 15	8 30	10 10	11 10	12 9	1 56	3 24	4 40	5 25	6 59	...
		dep.	5 55	8 16	8 40	10 11	11 11	12 10	1 57	3 25	4 50	5 26	7 0	...
4¾	Pidley-cum-Fenton Siding	,,		...	*	...	...	...	...	...	*	...	...	...
7	**Somersham**	arr.	6 10	8 26	9 0	10 21	11 21	12 20	2 7	3 35	5 15	5 36	7 10	...
	(G. N. and G. E. Joint)	dep.	...	...	...	...	...	...	...	...	6 0	...	...	...
12¼	St. Ives	arr.	...	...	...	...	...	...	...	...	6 15	...	...	...
			Mons only		Not Mons	Mons only								

A No. 1. Traffic for Pidley-cum-Fenton Siding to be taken to Warboys and be worked back by No. 3 Up Goods Train.
B Nos. 2 and 10. These Trains may work not exceeding 4 Trucks of important Goods or Cattle.

C No. 1. To attach or detach Traffic at Warboys if required.
D No. 11. This Train **may** work not exceeding 4 Trucks of important Goods or Cattle.

Working Timetable (GER) for June 1890

SOMERSHAM AND RAMSEY BRANCH.—*Single Line.*

(G.N. & G.E. Joint Line).

The Trains on this Single Line are worked by Train Staff and Train Staff Ticket, according to the " Train Staff Regulations " contained in the " Appendix " to this Working Time Book. No Engine or Train is to be run on this Branch without a Train Staff or Train Staff Ticket. The Train Staff Stations are Somersham, Warboys, and Ramsey.

Miles from Somersham.	DOWN TRAINS. Week Days.		1	2	3	4	5	6	7	8	9	10	11	12
			A Mxd	Pass.	Gds.	B Gds.	Eng.	Pass.	Pass.	C Pass.				
			a.m.	a.m.	p.m.	p.m.	p.m.	p.m.	p.m.	p.m.				
	St. Ives (G.E.)	dep.	...	...	...	1 35	2 20	...	...	6 33	...	...	...	...
—	**Somersham**	arr.	...	...	...	1 59	2 30	...	...	6 43	...	...	...	...
		dep.	9 12	11 41	12 30	2 0		2 35	5 5	6 44	...	...	...	...
2¼	Pidley-cum-Fenton Siding	,,	...	...	*		...	...	...	...	...	...	...	...
4¼	**Warboys**	arr.	9 23	11 50	12 50	2 10	...	2 44	5 14	6 53	...	...	...	...
		dep.	9 24	11 51	...	2 54	...	2 45	5 15	6 54	...	...	...	...
7	**Ramsey** (High Street)	arr.	9 30	11 57	...	3 0	...	2 51	5 21	7 0	...	...	...	...

Miles from Ramsey.	UP TRAINS. Week Days.		1	2	3	4	5	6	7	8	9	10	11	12
			Pass.	Pass.	Pass.	Pass.	Gds.	Eng.	Pass.	D Gds.	Mxd	Cars.		
			a.m.	a.m.	a.m.	p.m.	p.m.	p.m.	p.m.	p.m.	p.m.	p.m.		
—	**Ramsey** (High Street)	dep.	8 10	10 0	11 5	12 4	...	...	3 10	4 0	5 27	...	...	...
2¼	**Warboys**	arr.	8 15	10 5	11 10	12 9	...	...	3 15	4 6	5 33	...	...	...
		dep.	8 16	10 6	11 11	12 10	1 35	...	3 16	4 30	5 34	...	...	...
4¾	Pidley-cum-Fenton Siding	,,	...	...	...	...	*	...	...	*	...	...	...	...
7	**Somersham**	arr.	8 26	10 16	11 21	12 20	1 50	...	3 26	4 50	5 45	...	...	...
		dep.	...	...	...	...		2 0	...	5 30	...	6 0	...	...
12¼	St. Ives (G.E.)	arr.	...	...	...	...	...	2 10	...	5 45	...	6 12	...	...
				Mons only	Not Mons									

A No. 1. When necessary to attach or detach at Warboys, not exceeding 5 minutes extra time will be allowed at that Station and the Train will be due at Ramsey at 9.31 a.m.
B No. 4. May work Trucks from Somersham to Ramsey if required. From Ely at 10.45 a.m., via Sutton, see page 265. To shunt at Warboys for No. 5 Passenger Train.
C No. 8. May work Cattle from Somersham to Ramsey if Trucks are fitted with Break pipes.

D No. 8. Runs to Ely, via Sutton. See page 265.

Working Timetable (GER) 1897

From being a small fishing village, Skegness grew alarmingly with the arrival of its rail link, its population rising in the decade 1871–1881 from 349 to 1,332. On August Bank Holiday Monday 1882, 22,000 day trippers descended on the resort, pouring in from train after train, almost paralysing the station. All food shops in the town were sold out by 6.00 pm and such was the chaos caused by everyone wanting to get home at the same time that the last train did not get away until 2.30 the next morning, and even then hundreds of people were left behind. It was mostly Midlanders who patronised "Skeggy", but by the late 1880s the seaside habit had arrived even in land-locked Ramsey. A typical excursion train from the station in September 1888 to the delights of the Lincolnshire coastal resort left Ramsey at 8.20 am and arrived at Skegness at 10.35, giving Ramsey folk several hours to splash in the sea, stroll along the prom in the bracing breeze, or sample the advertised attractions of "the Switchback Railway and the Regatta" before returning home at 5.50 pm.

Hunstanton, the other favourite resort of northern East Anglians, had got off to a rather brisker start in the development of its tourist trade, having been reached by railway as early as 1862, the same year in which Edward, Prince of Wales, conferred Royal patronage on the area by buying nearby Sandringham House. By 1864 the Great Eastern had run its first cheap-day excursion from Huntingdon to what was called "the rising little watering-place" at a return fare of 3/-. By the time the Ramsey–Somersham line was opened, Hunstanton was firmly established as a busy resort for the folk of Norfolk, Cambridgeshire and Lincolnshire, and it was only a week after the branch's opening that a special train (carrying 43 passengers from Ramsey and 30 from Warboys) set off to the seaside, apparently in place of an excursion booked for Yarmouth the previous day which, for some reason, did not take place.

Ramsey's second branch line opened its services with a daily service of seven trains each way, with an extra train on Mondays, which was market day in St Ives. Perhaps by way of competition, the Holme branch timetable for July 1889, a couple of months before the Somersham line opened, showed an increase of passenger trains to a similar seven a day, leaving Ramsey at 7.15, 9.05, 9.50 am, 12.40, 3.35, 5.55, and 7.00 pm, with an additional Saturday-only service at 2.00 pm.

Once again it was agricultural produce and livestock which formed the staple goods traffic (it was a common sight to see queues of farm carts at the stations waiting to unload into railway wagons), supplemented significantly by consignments of bricks from Warboys. The large belts of clay which predominate in the Peterborough area

HOLME and RAMSEY.—Great Northern.

Miles	Week Days.	mrn	mrn	mrn	aft	aft	Sats. aft	Sats. aft	Sats. aft	Sats. aft	Sats. aft	
	Holme ....dep.	7 43	9 28	1042	1 14	2 31	3 47	4 e 8	4 18	8 33	9 15	....
3½	St. Mary's	7 54	9 37	1051	1 25	2 40	3 55	4e16	4 26	8 42	9 24	....
5½	Ramsey ** 302...arr.	7 59	9 40	1056	1 30	2 45	4 0	4e20	4 31	8 47	9 29	....

Miles	Week Days.	mrn	mrn	mrn	aft	aft	Sats. aft	Sats. aft	Sats. aft	Sats. aft	
	Ramsey ....dep.	7 0	9 10	9 45	1245	2 10	3 28	4 4	6 0	8 20	....
2	St. Mary's	7 7	9 15	9 50	1250	2 15	3 33	....	6 5	8 25	....
5½	Holme 342, 349 arr.	7 19	9 24	9 58	1259	2 24	3 41	4 14	6 14	8 34	....

e Except Saturdays. ** About ¼ mile to G.E. (High Street) Station.

SOMERSHAM and RAMSEY.—Great Eastern.

Miles	Week Days.	mrn	mrn	aft	non	aft	Mons. aft	Mons. aft	Mons. aft		
	Liverpool Street, 301London ....dep.	5 33	9 10	....	12 0	....	2 35	....	5 12	....	....
—	Somersham ....dep.	8 55	1144	1238	2 28	3 55	5 0	6 0	7 50	....	....
4½	Warboys	9 7	1154	1248	2 38	4 5	5 10	6 11	8 0	....	....
7	Ramsey (High St.) § 361	9 13	12 0	1254	2 44	4 11	5 16	6 17	8 6	....	....

Miles	Week Days.	mrn	mrn	Mons. mrn	Except Mons. aft	aft	aft	aft	Mons. aft	Mons. aft		
	High Street Station, Ramsey............dep.	8 10	10 0	11 5	12 7	1 40	3 19	4 16	5 24	7 0	....	....
2¼	Warboys................	8 16	10 6	1111	1213	1 46	3 25	4 23	5 30	7 7	....	....
7	Somersham 301....arr.	8 26	1016	1121	1223	1 56	3 35	4 33	5 40	7 18	....	....
83	301London (L'poolSt.) a	1056	....	....	2 49	....	6 6	....	8 26	....	....	....

§ About ¼ mile to Great Northern Station.

Somersham station in 1961 with the signal box seen in the distance. This replaced both the station and junction boxes in 1933. *D. Thompson*

RAMSEY AND HOLME BRANCH. NO SUNDAY TRAINS.

SINGLE LINE. TRAIN STAFF STATIONS. HOLME AND RAMSEY.

Distance from Holme (M)	(C)	DOWN	1 Gds. C	2 Mxd.	3 Pass.	4 Pass.	5 Mxd.	6 Mxd. Sats. only.		8 Pass. Sats. only.	Pass. Sats. Excpd. A	10 Pas. Sat. only. A	11 Lgt. engn.	12 Pass.	13 Gds.	14 Pass.		
M	C		a.m.	a.m.	a.m.	a.m.	p.m.	p.m.		p.m.	p.m.	p.m.	p.m.	p.m.	p.m.	p.m.		
...	...	HOLME ... dep.	5 58	7 43	9 28	10 42	1 14	2 31		3 47	4 9	4 18	5 37	6 33	7 56	9 15		
		St. Mary's ... arr.	6 10	...	...	...	...	...		...	...	...	...	...	...	...		
3	62	St. Mary's ... dep.	6 22	7 54	9 37	10 51	1 25	2 40		3 55	4 17	4 26	...	6 42	...	9 24		
5	65½	RAMSEY ... arr.	6 30	7 59	9 40	10 56	1 30	2 45		4 0	4 21	4 31	5 50	6 47	8 10	9 29		

Distance from Ramsey (M)	(C)	UP	1 Mxd	2 Pass.	3 Pass.	5 Pass.	6 Pass. Sats. only.		8 Pass.	9 Pass. Sats. only.	10 Goods. Sats. expd.	10 Goods. Sats. only.		11 Pass.	12 Gds.	13 Pass.	14 Lgt. Eng. D		
M	C		a.m.	a.m.	a.m	p.m.	p.m.		p.m.	p.m.	p.m.	p.m.		p.m.	p.m.	p.m.	p.m.		
...	...	RAMSEY ... dep.	7 0	9 10	9 45	12 45	2 10	...	3 28	4 4	4 35	4 40	...	6 0	7 5	8 15	9 35	...	...
		St. Mary's ... arr.	...	...	...	...	...	...	...	...	4 41	4 46	...	...	7 11	...	...	...	...
2	3¼	St. Mary's ... dep.	7 7	9 15	9 50	12 50	2 15	...	3 33	...	5 5	5 10	...	6 5	7 31	8 20	...	...	...
5	65¼	HOLME ... arr.	7 19	9 24	9 58	12 59	2 24	...	3 41	4 14	5 17	5 22	...	6 14	7 41	8 29	9 50	...	...

A May take cattle if wagons are fitted with brake pipes.
C From New England, see train 106, page 66.
D To New England see train 761, page 43.

Working Timetable for 1910

Holme Station buildings seen here in April 1957 with the branch line on the extreme right of the picture. *D. Thompson*

and stretch down to Bedfordshire, and which gave rise to a large concentration of brickworks in the nineteenth century, thrust a number of small outcrops into the peaty acreage of the Fens. Brick-making was already in existence in a small, domestic way at Ramsey Heights in the middle of the century: "Kelly's Directory" for 1854 records two local men engaged in the trade, although both had other occupations as well, one as a farmer and the other as a beer retailer. Brick-making on a larger, more organised scale came to the Ramsey area when one of the Directors of the Ramsey–Somersham railway, Alfred Fuller, opened a brick and tile-making works, with three kilns, alongside the line at Warboys station in 1893, producing the unique Warboys White bricks of a type and colour found nowhere else in the country. A similar, but smaller, works, with only one kiln, was built nearer to Somersham Junction at about the same time and was referred to variously as the Somersham Brick Company or the Pidley Brick Company. Both of these works had rail access; indeed, the smaller complex was accessible only by rail. Brick-making flourished in the couple of decades after the establishment of the works, and by the early 1920s the first goods working of the day on the branch was designated specifically for brick traffic, an engine leaving Ramsey East at 6.00 am to pick up loaded wagons from Warboys to take on to the yard at Somersham where they would be dropped off for later despatch to their various destinations; the engine meanwhile would return to Ramsey with any incoming freight, and was then ready to work the first outgoing passenger train of the day, which left Ramsey at about 7.30 am.

The two branch lines were worked in slightly different ways, consequent on the differing facilities which each terminus offered. Although Ramsey North was originally provided with an engine shed, and presumably therefore could retain an engine overnight ready for the first morning departure, this shed had disappeared by the turn of the century, and thereafter engines had to work in to the station before any other stock movement could take place. The usual pattern of working was that an early morning freight would leave Peterborough, reverse at Holme and take any loaded wagons for St Mary's and Ramsey North. After the wagons had been shunted off at the terminus the engine would then pick up the empty coaching stock (which, well into this century, were often ancient, gas-lighted six-wheelers) which had been stabled at Ramsey overnight, to form the first passenger departure of the day. In the evening, the process was reversed, with coaches from the last passenger train being left at Ramsey while freight wagons were returned, together with the engine, to Peterborough.

Ramsey East, on the other hand, retained an engine shed for much longer than its neighbouring station, and could therefore keep its own locomotive permanently on supply. In the late 1920s, for example, engines 8308 and 8310, of class F7, were allocated to Ramsey on a weekly rota: while one was working the branch, the other was returned to Cambridge depot for boiler wash-out and any running repairs that might be necessary. These 2–4–2 tank engines, built by the Great Eastern in 1909–10 for light branch line duties and push-pull workings, had such large cabs in comparison to their small boilers that enginemen nicknamed them "Crystal Palaces" in tribute to their imposing superstructure. Possession of an engine shed meant that, in addition to its two sets of drivers and firemen, Ramsey East could afford to employ its own engine cleaner, whose jobs included coaling and lighting up the engine, using wood sent in wagonloads from Stratford Carriage and Wagon Works; keeping the shed clean (the windows were washed regularly every week); and keeping the coaling stage supplied with coal unloaded by hand from a truck, at an overtime rate of eightpence-halfpenny a ton.

Although freight traffic continued in a very healthy condition on both branches, passenger traffic on the Ramsey–Somersham line showed a steady decline, and in 1922 the station office at Warboys was closed down, a straw in the wind which heralded the full-scale withdrawal of passenger services a few years later.

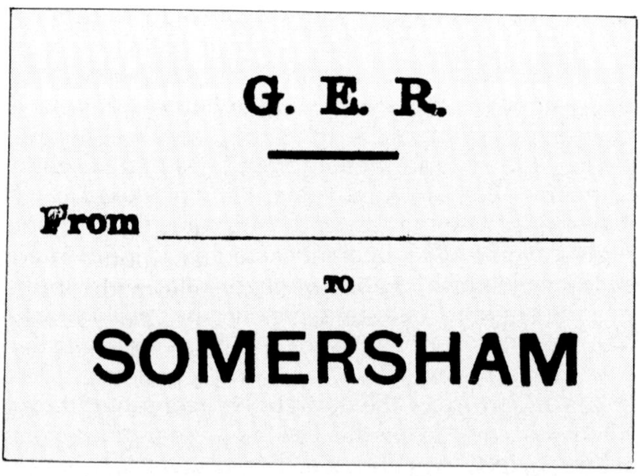
G. E. R.

From ______________

TO

SOMERSHAM

Chapter 4

From Grouping to Closure

Under the 1923 Grouping plans Ramsey's two formerly rival branch lines found themselves united under the ownership of the newly-created LNER. Within a few months it was being rumoured that the new Company was looking into the possibility of reviving the old idea of linking the two systems to provide a through route, a move which, it was felt, would make the lines much more economically viable than if they continued to exist as separate branches. Whether the LNER did, in fact, consider this I have been unable to confirm, but if the authorities did indeed look closely at the profitability of the two routes they arrived at a very different conclusion from the one some Ramsey inhabitants expected.

By the end of the 1920s, road transport was beginning to make its presence felt in an increasingly decisive way. Lorries belonging to small local haulage firms were becoming a more and more familiar sight, acting not only as feeders to the railway system but in direct competition with it, competition that was highly effective with the sort of door-to-door service a lorry could provide. Private cars, although still in relatively small numbers, were rapidly increasing in popularity as mass production brought down the price and opened up a wider market. The railways, hitherto in possession of a virtual monopoly of transport, suddenly found themselves faced with vigorous competition and the consequent need to rationalise their own sprawling system of routes.

By this time the Somersham branch passenger service was down to four trains a day, half its former strength, and even these were often lightly loaded. Occasionally well-patronised trains, such as the one run in the late 1920s which carried the Somersham football team and its crowd of supporters to a local Cup-tie derby against Ramsey, were not enough to convince anyone that the line was paying its way, and the LNER eventually decided that two routes into Ramsey was a luxury that it could not afford to continue. At this time, long before the 1947 Transport Act which laid down statutory procedures for advising of closure and the setting-up of an inquiry to hear any objections, the process of closure was entirely in the hands of the owning company, and, accordingly, it was a bare announcement (dated 4th September, 1930) in the local press and on station notice-boards that closure was imminent that first brought the matter to the notice of the population of the Ramsey and Somersham areas. The 22nd September was the date set for withdrawal of all passenger services, with a promise of a substitute bus service to be provided by the Eastern National Omnibus Company. Freight traffic would

SOMERSHAM and RAMSEY.—Great Eastern.

Miles	Down.	Week Days only. mrn	mrn	noon	aft	aft
	245 London (Liverpool Street) dep.	5 53	8 30	12J0	2 34	....
	245 " (St. Pancras) ..... "	....	....	....	....	....
—	Somersham ....dep.	9 14	1118	2 19	5 4	8 5
4½	Warboys	9 26	1128	2 29	5 14	6 15
7	Ramsey (High Street) * 298a arr.	9 33	1134	2 35	5 20	6 21

Miles	Up.	Week Days only. mrn	mrn (Mons. only.)	mrn (Except Mons.)	aft	aft	aft
	Ramsey (High Street)........dep.	7 28	10 0	1026	1 0	3 5	5 30
2½	Warboys	7 44	10 6	1032	1 6	3 12	5 36
7	Somersham 245 ....arr.	7 54	1016	1042	1 16	3 24	5 46
83¼	245 London (St. Pancras).....arr.	....	....	....	....	....	....
83	245 " (Liverpool Street) "	1023	2 7	2 7	5 9	6 10	8 33

Passenger Timetable 1921

remain: it was expected that two goods trains a day would use the line, and a special engine and brakevan would be sent regularly to Warboys from Cambridge to convey produce from Warboys to the London area.

Ironically, and as if to underline the growing threat of road transport, at the same time as the withdrawal notice was issued a British-built Chevrolet truck, fully loaded, did an exhibition run for seven days and nights non-stop, covering a total of 3,568 miles, starting from Peterborough and following a circular route almost alongside the railway through Ramsey, Warboys, and Somersham, returning to Peterborough via March and Whittlesey.

Little interest seems to have been aroused by the withdrawal of passenger services: apart from the official withdrawal notice itself, I have been unable to find any reports or comments in the local newspapers; even the final day of passenger operations remains officially unchronicled, although private photographic evidence indicates that the very last passenger train, of a modest two coaches, was worked by Ramsey East's 'F7' No. 8308. With the end of this service, Ramsey East's engine shed was shut down, and the two engine crews and cleaner formerly employed here were transferred, together with their engines, to Cambridge.

The Eastern National's replacement bus service proved not to be satisfactory in all respects, some difficulty being experienced in connecting with the still-existing rail service at Somersham. The ex-

Cambridge train which used to arrive at Somersham at about 4.45 pm, for example, was so tightly timed in conjunction with the bus service that if it was even a few minutes late the bus driver had to decide whether to wait for it at Somersham station or set off for Ramsey, since his bus was due back in Somersham to make connection with another train some time before 6.00 pm. If he did wait, and was consequently late on the return trip, he might well miss the train by just a few minutes. It was possible to see Somersham station from some distance away as one approached by road, and there are reports of late buses covering the last mile or so to the station at break-neck speed and with hooter blaring to prevent the train leaving too early!

From the time that the Somersham line lost its passenger service, the history of both branch lines shows a steady decline in the face of road competition, and, apart from a resurgence of business during the war years, when the railways were once again able to show their ability to carry people and materials in large quantities, the writing on the wall became plainer, and its message more unmistakable. An official LNER report of 1928, for example, indicated the way in which a former rival form of transport, the inland waterway, had declined in importance but had been replaced by the much more serious threat of the motor vehicle. In the section of the report which concerned the Ramsey area waterways it was stated that:

> In the vicinity of Holme the Midland Level Drainage Commissioners do not consider navigation a primary consideration and the water level is so low that during the past two or three years traffic has not been boated to Holme Wharf in appreciable quantities, though we get it both by road and by boat at St Mary's. At Ramsey North very little traffic is boated for either local mills or rail transit.

On the other hand,

> bearing in mind the fact that roads in country districts are now in much better condition, whilst many farmers possess motor lorries of their own and there are also many road motor haulage companies in existence, it seems to us that the fear of water competition is nothing like the same as in 1902, our principal enemy now being road transport.

This transition period, when road and rail transport seemed to be evenly balanced in their attempts to win traffic, is neatly exemplified by the situation at Warboys brickworks in the mid-1930s. By this time the works had been taken over by the London Brick Company and Forders Ltd, who had extensive yards also at nearby Fletton. A recent boom in brick-making consequent on a large number of new housing schemes had meant considerable activity at Warboys: 60 men (and

A New England "Flying Pig", class 4MT, 2–6–0 on the Ramsey North branch at Holme Fen in 1962. *Peterborough Railway Society Collection*

one very aged cat named Felix, the yard mascot) were employed digging clay from the pit, or "knot-hole", entirely by hand. Production was 300,000 bricks a week, or 15 million a year, most of these being despatched to the Cambridge area. Significantly, however, most of this traffic was now being carried by lorry rather than by train, although the railway was continuing to carry large quantities of agricultural produce, as evidenced, for example, by the lines of wagons loaded with sugarbeet regularly seen in Warboys sidings.

The mid-30s were, in fact, a time when the railways even seemed to be winning back some of the ground lost to road transport at the end of the previous decade. In the ten years following Grouping the total freight business of the LNER fell by 45m. tons. By 1933 a 9% increase in freight had replaced the 8% drop of the previous year, but although this trend was maintained for a brief time, by the outbreak of war it was clear that the railways were again falling behind rapidly. By 1939 East Anglia alone contained 50,000 motor goods vehicles operated by 17,000 separate owners, mostly small local firms such as

WEEKDAYS **SOMERSHAM AND WARBOYS**

Mileage M	Mileage C	DOWN			K 11.55 am from Whitemoor		Mileage M	Mileage C	UP				F To Whitemoor
					SX								SX
					PM								PM
0	0	SOMERSHAM	arr	.....	1 29	.....	0	0	Warboys	dep	.....	.....	2 55
		.. .. ..	dep	..	1 55	..	2	11	Pidley-cum-Fenton Siding ..	..	..	..	R
2	20	Pidley-cum-Fenton Siding	.....	.....	.....	.....	4	31	SOMERSHAM	arr	.....	.....	3 28
4	31	Warboys..	arr	..	2 15				.. ..	dep	..	..	3 55

Working Timetable BR(ER) 1961

Loughs of Ramsey, whose proprietors are shown in a photograph taken in 1936 (and now in possession of the Huntingdon Record Office) posing proudly alongside their gleaming new lorry, parked, ironically, outside "The Railway Arms"! To underline the danger that was posed to passenger services as well, a survey for the same year (1939) showed that for the whole of Suffolk the estimated number of rail passenger tickets collected was only 21,000 in January and 97,000 in August, the peak holiday month. The Somersham–Ramsey branch reflected this decline particularly: not only had it already lost its passenger service, but its freight traffic took a knock with the successive closure of the Somersham gravel works in about 1935, only a few years after their opening, and the Warboys brickworks at the beginning of the war.

The Holme branch, on the other hand, had undergone some cosmetic treatment. After the withdrawal of the Somersham passenger service the LNER had clearly decided to improve the standard of running and maintenance for the Holme trains, and had embarked on a programme of renewal and replacement. Some stretches of track, threatened by the ever-present subsidence, were relaid, newer signalling equipment was installed, and some new sidings were provided at Ramsey North. There was, however, a tacit warning that this was only a refurbishing exercise and was not heralding a new and illustrious future for the line: a 15 mph speed restriction was imposed on all branch trains. By this time, the Holme passenger service was

Class C12, 4–4–2T, a locomotive type frequently seen on the Holme to Ramsey branch. Seen here at Stamford East in the 1950s. *Lens of Sutton*

Class F7 (2–4–2T) No. 8306, seen here at Stratford in March 1927. These engines were regular motive power on the Somersham to Ramsey branch lines. *H.C. Casserley*

being progressively pruned, and by 1938 there were only three trains a day each way, and, by a peculiar and highly inconvenient piece of timetabling, all in the morning: it was now impossible to reach Ramsey by rail after 10.15 am.

Just as it seemed as if the railways would inevitably succumb to the persistent pressure of road competition, the war intervened to swing things back in favour of the rail companies, now combined under government control. With severe petrol rationing and the hazards of the blackout, motoring became a difficult business, and many family saloons spent the war years stowed away in garages, propped up on blocks and cocooned in cobwebs. The railways, in their unique capacity as bulk carriers, were undoubtedly a vital element in the mass movement of materials for the war effort, and a lifeline for those people who needed to get about the country on business or pleasure (although there was little of the latter, with trains often crowded to capacity, and a vigorous government advertising campaign asking "Is your journey really necessary?").

The eastern counties, because of their proximity to Europe, were already patchworked with operational airfields, and many more were built to accommodate the thousands of bombers and fighters turned out by the munitions industry. There were two airfields in the immediate vicinity of Ramsey, and the necessity to keep these supplied with essential materials provided a great increase in the freight traffic on both branch lines. Upwood aerodrome, to the south-west of Ramsey, had been established as long ago as 1917 (only five years after the formation of the Royal Flying Corps) as a base for two night-training squadrons, whose stick-and-string machines droned monotonously around the local skies for a couple of years until, with the ending of the war, the squadrons were disbanded and the airfield reverted to farmland and its original rural quietness. With the preparations for another likely war, the base was rebuilt in January 1937 and became home for two light bomber squadrons, once again with training as its object. In late 1943 concrete runways were laid, and Mosquitos and Lancasters of 2 Pathfinder Squadron made Upwood their home; during its operational period, from February 1944 to the end of the war, 6,000 sorties were mounted from the base, including a series of 36 consecutive night attacks when Lancaster bombers, heavy with their deadly loads, took off to raid Berlin. There was some retaliation, however: Upwood itself was attacked by enemy raiders on half a dozen occasions but suffered no real damage, although in a raid in the spring of 1940 one person was killed. The second of the Ramsey area's airfields was a smaller affair, situated to the south-west of Warboys, and also used as a bomber base during the war.

Two operational bases meant that, in addition to constant movement of RAF personnel, large supplies of aviation fuel, spare parts, bombs and ammunition needed to be brought in regularly by rail. At the beginning of the war a further new siding was installed at Ramsey North specifically for the handling of ammunition trains, whose sheeted wagons carried red-flashed labels warning of the dangers of such volatile cargo: "SHUNT WITH GREAT CARE" and "Place as far as possible from engine, brake-van and wagons labelled INFLAMMABLE". The ever-present danger of handling this kind of train was brought home to train crews in a devastating way in June 1944 when at Soham, not too many miles distant from Ramsey, one wagon on a train conveying bombs caught fire and exploded, flattening Soham station and damaging 700 houses in the village.

The end of the war meant a rapid disappearance of this type of traffic on the two branch lines: Warboys airfield, after doing duty as a P.O.W. camp through 1946 and 1947, was closed down, and part of it utilised for an extension to the local cemetery; and although Upwood airfield remained open for flying until 1961, it no longer needed to be supplied by rail in the same way as during the war. Brick traffic, however, picked up again with the reopening of the works at Warboys as part of the national drive for reconstruction of bomb-damaged towns and cities, and was soon in full production, with trains of up to 40 loaded wagons leaving the sidings on occasions.

Ramsey's remaining passenger service, however, had begun to decline still further, particularly without the volume of traffic that the airfields had supplied, and was now down to three trains a day, the earliest at 6.50 am for connection with the 10.15 arrival at Kings Cross, and the latest at 8.00 pm for travellers who left London on the 4.50. Only the early morning train now called at St Mary's. Sceptical about the continuing viability of the line's passenger-carrying capability, the LNER commissioned a survey in 1946 to establish the actual number of people using the branch. The results were depressing: the best-loaded train only carried nine people, and a comparison of pre-war and post-war figures showed that, whereas in 1931 14,000 passengers had used Ramsey North station, in 1946 there had only been 2,665, a drop of 80%. Parcels traffic, it was revealed, was also in decline. It came as no real surprise, therefore, when the LNER announced that passenger services would be withdrawn from 6th October, 1947.

Although Ramsey had taken the removal of its first branch-line passenger service apparently without protest, the prospect of being left without a rail link of any kind was sufficient to stir up some vocal opposition: in a picturesque simile the *Hunts Post* likened Ramsey

The RCTS Fensman Special Railtour on Sunday, 24th July, 1955, seen here at Ramsey East with 0–6–0, No. 65562, in charge. *E.H. Sawford*

The RCTS Fensman, with supporters at Ramsey East on 24th July, 1955. *E.H. Sawford*

The "R.E.C. Charnwood Forester" special seen here at St Mary's on its way to Ramsey. *C. Gammell*

people to children who have suddenly had their toffee apples snatched away, only to realise that there was still some toffee left on them! A commonly expressed complaint was that the isolation consequent on the rail service being taken away would be detrimental to Ramsey's population, who would be "unable to get out of the place", as one local put it, and to some local businesses which relied on the passenger rather than the freight service. Morning newspapers, for example, normally delivered by early passenger train, would not in future arrive in Ramsey until 10.00 am, which would be too late for them to be sorted and delivered before mid-afternoon or even early evening. The lack of convenient connections at Holme, and the generally poor standard of service represented by the few remaining trains, was cited as a reason for the scarcity of support shown by Ramsey people, and a suggestion was made that passengers could be attracted back to the line if an hourly rail-car service, like those in use on some GWR branches, were put into operation. The vice-chairman of Ramsey Urban Council was blunt in his condemnation of the way the LNER pruned off uneconomic parts of their system with apparent disregard for their obligations to the travelling public: "We contend that the Company are supposed to give a service to the public and they should regard their receipts only from the point of view of the final result spread over the whole system". In other words, the LNER should be prepared to subsidise loss-making lines from the profits made by successful routes.

A meeting of Ramsey tradesmen on 24th September went so far as to write formally to the LNER stating that if services were to be reprieved they could guarantee that they would be well supported, particularly in view of the fact that private motoring was affected by the rationing of petrol which was still in force. Such bland assurance cut no ice with the railway company, however in a letter to the Ramsey UDC, read out at a meeting held on the day after closure took place, the LNER repeated that the line had been losing money for a considerable time, and that now "there was no prospect of the service ever paying its way". Withdrawal of passenger trains, it was said, would save £2,450, and 200 tons of coal, a year.

There were some cynical murmurings that closure had been contrived for reasons of convenience to the Company: the LNER's reminder in its closure notices that an adequate substitute bus service would be provided by the Eastern Counties Bus Company brought the comment that it was more than coincidental that the LNER had holdings in this Company; and at least one person took the opportunity to blame the whole thing in some obscure way on the approaching process of nationalisation, already authorised, and due to take effect from 1st January, 1948. There were complaints about the validity of the census taken by the LNER to establish the line's lack of profitability: a time was deliberately chosen, it was suggested, when many people, including some rail staff, were away on holiday.

Although the local M.P., David Renton, launched a campaign to keep the line open, the truth of the LNER's assertion about the passenger service was demonstrated by the final day's services. The last train from Holme, at 10.15 am on 6th October, carried precisely three passengers, all described as "railway enthusiasts", two of whom were not even local, but who had travelled from London just for the occasion. At St Mary's the booking office was opened specially so that they could purchase souvenir tickets. No such concessions were made at Ramsey North, where the ticket-hatch was already firmly barred by a board proclaiming "Issue no more tickets". Ramsey people were conspicuous by their absence: "Little interest was shown in the event", a newspaper report stated tersely.

Ramsey North on 14th April, 1957, with a special excursion arriving. The engine is a class C12, No. 67380, in charge of the "R.E.C. Charnwood Forester" special. *H.C. Casserley*

The Cambridge University Railway Club excursion on the daily freight service from Peterborough to Ramsey North. Seen here arriving at Ramsey behind class 08 diesel shunter No. D3449 in March 1964. *Paul Slater*

Ramsey's two branch lines, then, entered nationalised ownership under British Railways as freight-only lines, worked largely by 'J15s' or 'J17s', and still carrying predominantly agricultural produce such as grain, seed, potatoes and sugarbeet. The Friday afternoon goods train provided some variation, in that as well as picking up freight it also carried in its brakevan the Somersham station master, whose duty it was on this day to deliver pay-packets to his staff at Warboys and Ramsey East.

Passenger working did return briefly to the Somersham branch, however, when a special train organised by the RCTS and hauled by 'J17' No. 65562 made a visit on 24th July, 1955 to Ramsey East as part of an enthusiasts railtour. For a few years during the early 1950s a once-yearly passenger train ran an excursion to Yarmouth Races, usually 'B1'-hauled, and with as many as eight coaches, an impressively long train by branch-line standards. Even this infrequent service was soon brought to an end by a decision in 1956 to close down the Ramsey East-Warboys section of line, since the amount of freight no longer justified continued operation. Closure was effective from 17th September.

Little more, in fact, remains to be said about the Somersham branch: with brick traffic now predominantly road-hauled, the four and a half mile stub between Somersham and Warboys became more and more uneconomical to work, only one goods train a day using the branch. This train would originate from March, leaving at about 11.30 am, and call at Wimblington and Chatteris *en route* to Somersham, arriving at about 1.30 pm to drop wagons in the yard and collect any wagons destined for Warboys. Progress along the branch was sedate, a maximum 15 mph, with stops to operate the crossing gates at Pidley and the A141 road (crossing-keepers having been dispensed with some years ago), and arrival at Warboys was some 15 or 20 minutes after leaving Somersham. At the entrance to the loop in Warboys station, the engine would be uncoupled and run into the left-hand platform; since the station was on a gradient the wagons were then allowed to roll under their own momentum into the goods platform where they were then shunted, and the crew paused for a dinner break. On the return trip, Pidley Siding was shunted if required, although this became an increasingly rare occurrence, and the train arrived back at Somersham at about 4.00 pm ready for leave for March. Sometimes there would be only a single truck of coal for Warboys, and this was then propelled along the branch. The occasions when there was not even a single truck-load for Warboys became more and more frequent, and eventually and inevitably closure of the branch came on 13th July, 1964, when all services

With engine and station staff posed around locomotive No. 8308 and its two
coach train, this view shows the final trip from Somersham to Warboys and

ceased. For a time, before track was lifted, the redundant line was used for the storage of empty coal wagons. The line had been steam-worked up until about August 1962, class J17 No. 65576 being the last steam engine to work it, after which class 31 diesels from March carried out most of the operations.

The Holme–Ramsey line, although now closed to passengers, was visited on 14th April, 1957 by a special enthusiasts train, "The Charnwood Forester", organised by the Railway Enthusiasts Club of Farnborough as part of an extensive railtour covering Stamford, Market Harborough, Glenfield, Shepshed, Nuneaton, Bedford and Hitchin. Originating from Kings Cross, the tour was 'A4'-hauled as far as Holme, where a Peterborough-based 'C12' 4–4–2T No. 67380 took the five coaches on to Ramsey, pausing at St Mary's for five minutes *en route* for photographs. The 'C12s', an H.A. Ivatt design of 1898, were very much at home on this line, having been used extensively in earlier years for passenger workings; by this time, however, they were on their way out, only about 20 remaining. (Another one of the class, No. 67357, later in the day took the railtour on the Essendine to Stamford section of the route.)

By now, there were signs of deterioration in the track on the branch. The old bugbear, shrinkage of the peat subsoil, had produced continued subsidence in many places so that there were stretches where the riding was akin to that of a switchback; speed restrictions at some locations, such as over the small trestle bridge near St Mary's, had had to be dropped to 10 mph. As part of economy measures introduced in the late 1950s and early 1960s, all signals at St Mary's were removed, and gatekeepers employed at the few level crossings were dispensed with. Henceforth, gates were to be opened and closed by train crews, warning signs being erected to remind them of the approach to a crossing at 440 yds on either side. From 2nd May, 1960 St Mary's ceased to be manned at all and became an unstaffed public delivery siding (having lost its goods yard some time before) which would continue to deal with any produce, such as potatoes, which local farmers were still willing to bring in. A couple of men were still retained at Ramsey North for freight handling, however, since coal traffic to the Peterborough Co-operative Society's sidings remained heavy.

By early 1964, steam haulage had almost disappeared from the branch, in the latter years having been predominantly in the capable charge of New England-based 4MT class 2–6–0s. It was one of these engines that worked the first of two special branch-line trains for the Cambridge University Railway Club in March 1964, when a couple of extra brakevans were added to the daily Peterborough–Ramsey freight for the conveyance of the enthusiasts. The ride must have been far from comfortable, since at Holme a lengthy session of shunting was indulged in with wagons from both up and down yards, with various bone-shaking manœuvres across the main lines before jolting off up the weed-grown branch to Ramsey. The second trip, a week later, was worked by class 08 diesel shunter D3449, but sounds as if it was just as physically exhausting.

The Holme branch successfully completed its century in 1963 and, perhaps contrary to many expectations, managed to survive into the 1970s. St Mary's eventually vanished from the railway map in February 1972, when its delivery siding was closed down, but a single daily goods train, trailing a few mineral wagons, continued to visit Ramsey North until July 1973, when Ramsey's rail link was eventually withdrawn for good. Track, station buildings, and level crossings remained *in situ* for a year or so, gradually decaying or disappearing under encroaching weeds and bushes. In September 1974 Ramsey station was levelled, and the site more or less cleared; at the end of the year the six miles of track were lifted. The ensuing decade has seen some of the trackbed return to a natural state, or vanish entirely under ploughing or construction; however, enough has survived to enable anyone to follow the course of the line, and these remains are detailed in the final chapter of this book.

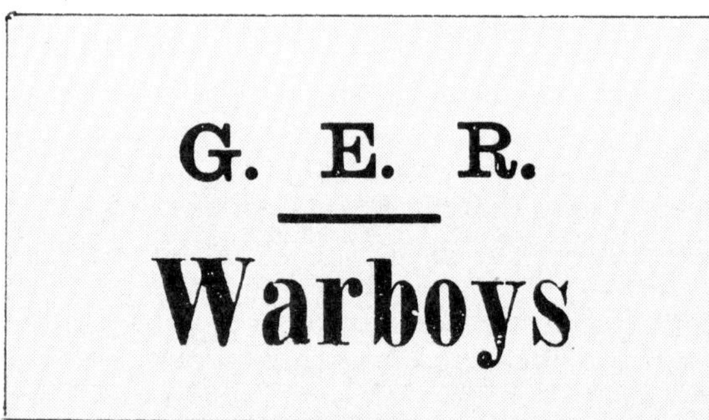
G. E. R.

Warboys

Chapter 5

The Route and its Remains

Holme–Ramsey

A couple of years after the completion of the GN main line between Kings Cross and Peterborough in 1850, the small station at Holme was opened as part of the policy of providing stations where there might be the remotest chance of attracting traffic. Holme at this time was a mere hamlet, but the station facilities were reasonably comprehensive: two platforms, one an island, a signal box and level crossing, and a goods yard on the down side of the main double track. With the completion of the Ramsey branch in 1863 Holme station was slightly modified in accordance with its new status as a junction. Since branch trains were to use the eastward face of the island platform, a separate set of crossing gates, worked by station staff under instructions from the signalman, was provided for the single track across the Holme–Ramsey road (now the B660). A connecting crossover was provided between branch line and up and down main lines at the north end of the station, and goods loading facilities were installed on the up side, opposite the existing goods yard.

The Ramsey branch ran parallel to the GN main line for about 400 yards as it left Holme station (entry to the branch was protected by one of the distinctive GN somersault signals, which remained in use until the very end of the line's existence) and then curved sharply eastwards, the line being fitted with a check rail on this curve, skirting a large wood and striking out across the flat expanse of Holme Fen. At Whittlesey Mere Crossing (the name being a reminder of the fact that this part of the line was built on the edge of the drained Whittlesey Mere) the line crossed a minor road, New Long Drove, necessitating a single set of crossing gates in the charge of a crossing-keeper, who was provided with a brick-built house and small garden. Similar facilities were found at Long Drove Crossing, a mile or so further on, as the line began to turn slightly southwards, crossing the road at quite an acute angle. Now in the middle of open fields, the railway approached the old course of the river Nene, which it crossed by an iron bridge of three spans supported on two iron columns sunk into the river bed. This bridge was a frail-looking structure, not much wider than the single line of railway, with no guard rails at the side, and in later years, because of the subsidence of the trackbed at either end, it gave every appearance of being slightly hump-backed, being approached by quite marked gradients.

Three and three-quarter miles from Holme was the branch's only intermediate station, the small halt at St Mary's. With the draining and reclamation of Ramsey Mere and Ugg Mere in the nineteenth

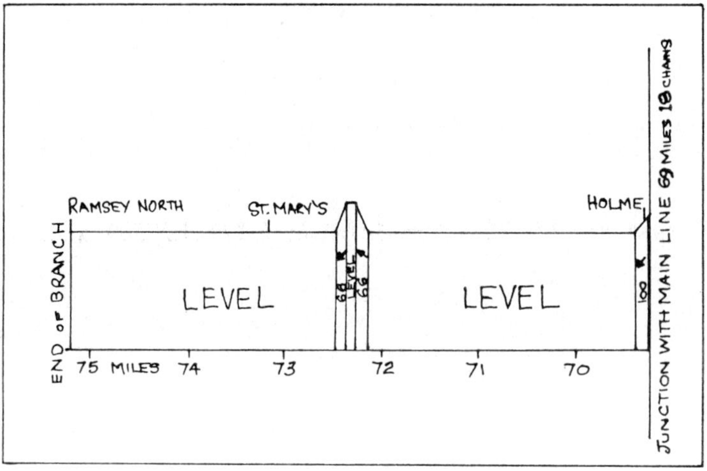

Gradient Profile for Holme to Ramsey North

Holme Station in 1936, looking south. This photograph shows the level crossing and signal box. The goods train is on the down main line with the Ramsey Branch engine shunting in the background. On the left is the waiting shelter on the up platform. Beyond this island platform can be seen the water tank, engine column and loading gauge with LMS open wagons in the far distance. *Lens of Sutton*

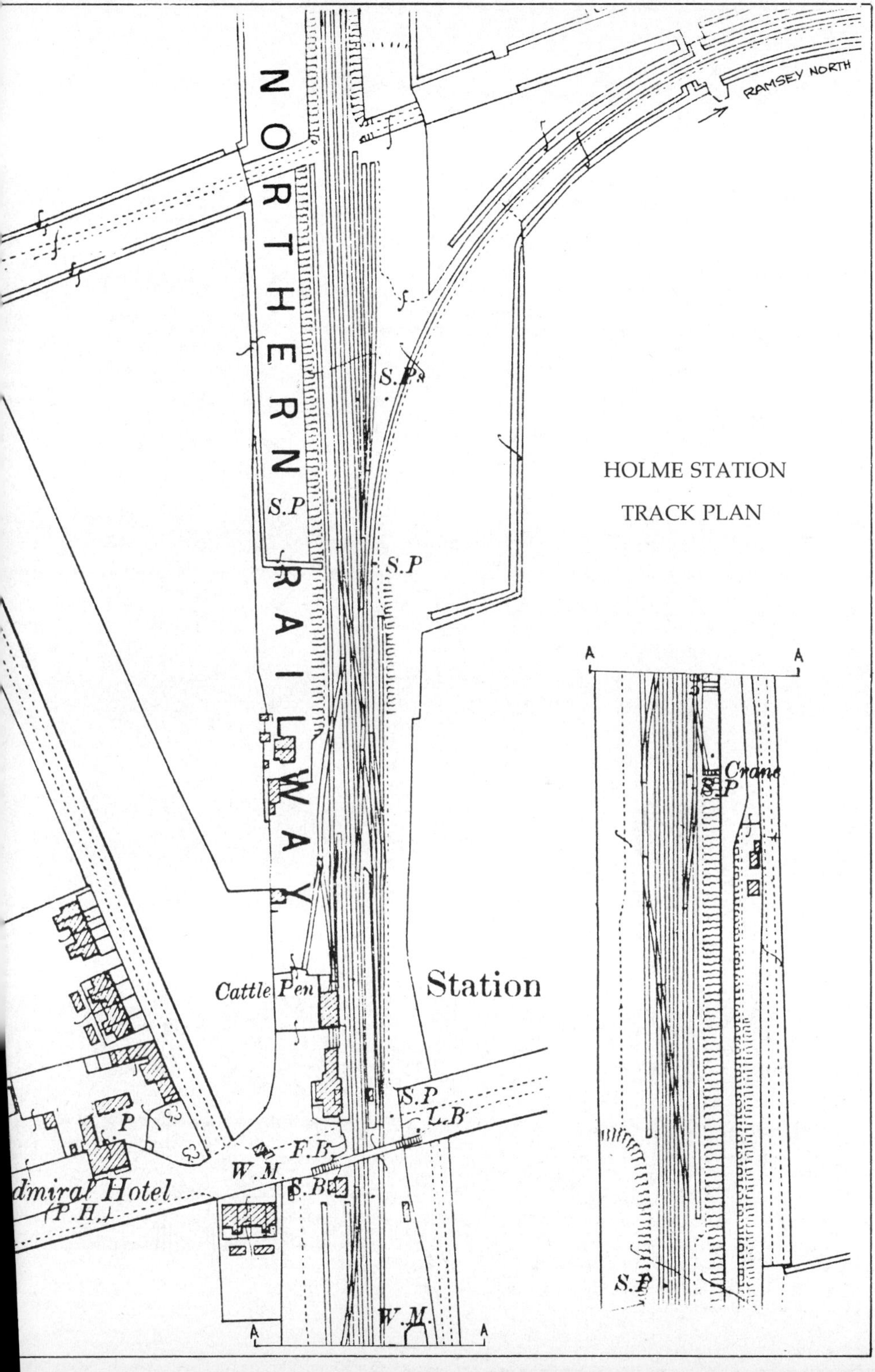

HOLME STATION

TRACK PLAN

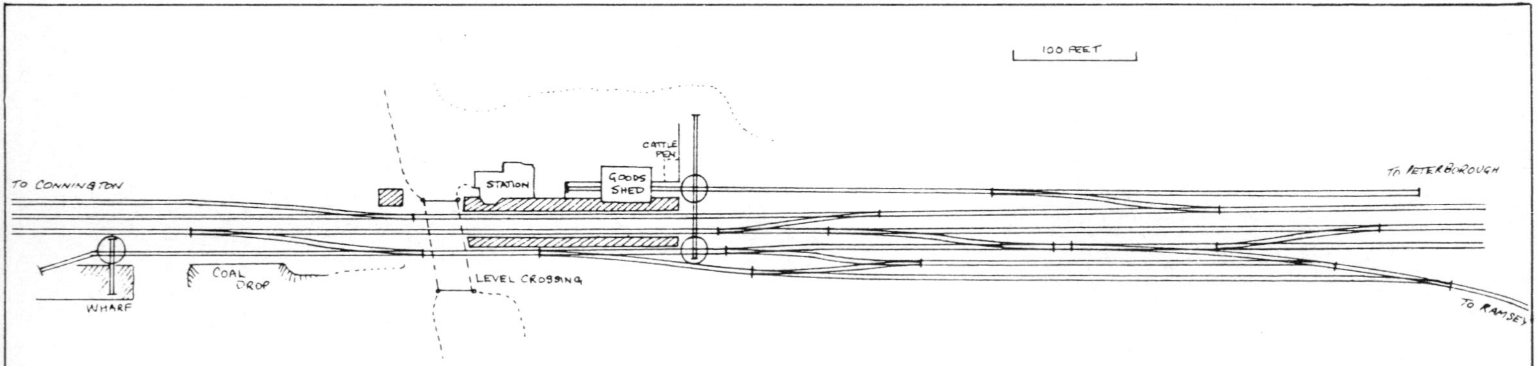

HOLME STATION (1860s LAYOUT)

An early 1930s photograph taken at Holme. The station nameboard shows the change for the branch and the Class J6, 0–6–0 No. 3528, waits at the branch platform with a NE "perishable" box van, used for parcel traffic on the branch.
Lens of Sutton

St Mary's unstaffed goods station seen here in 1964, looking towards Ramsey. The level crossing with large lamp can clearly be seen. Although the siding for the goods dock has been removed, the brick goods transit shed remains.
Lens of Sutton

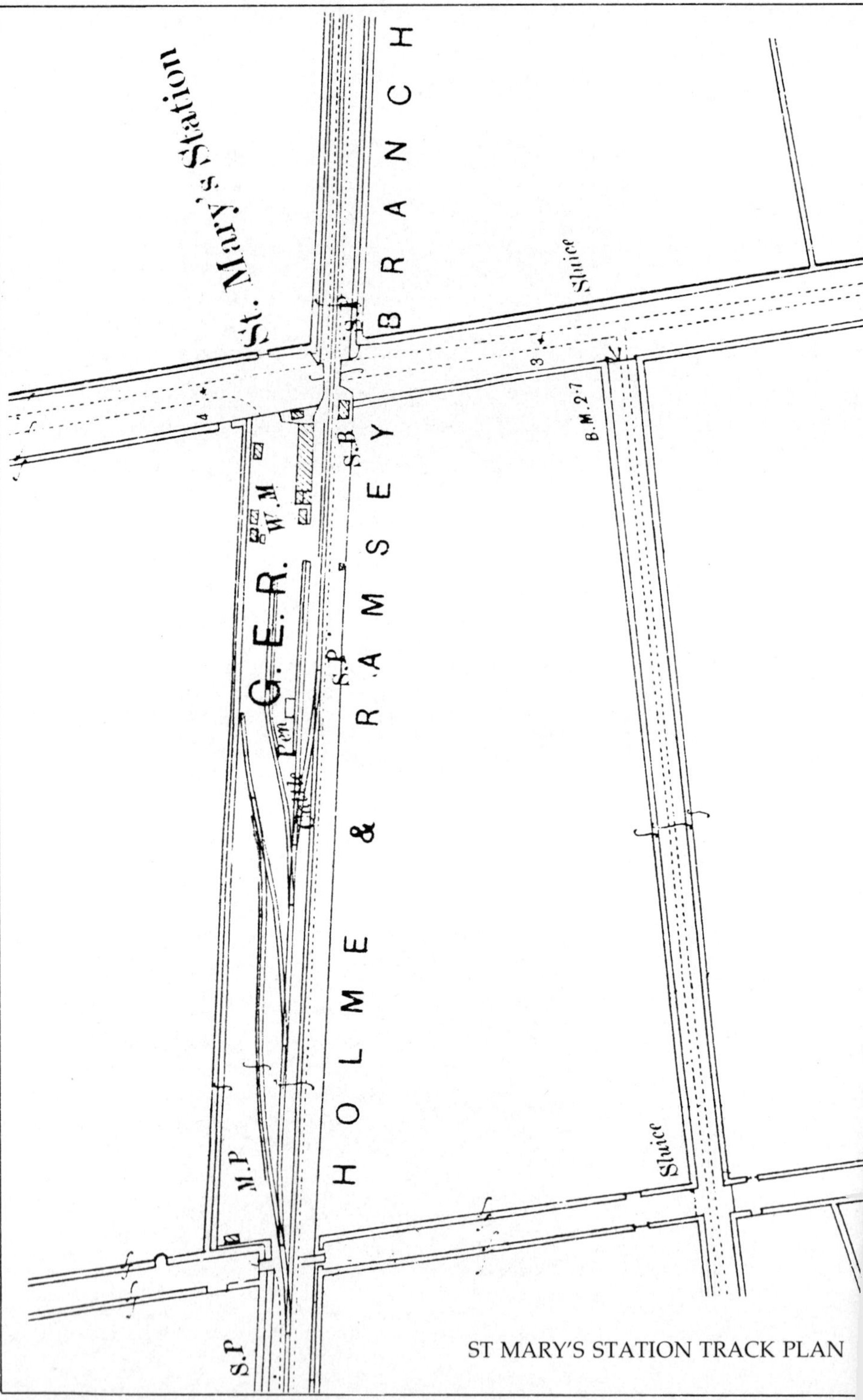

ST MARY'S STATION TRACK PLAN

Ramsey North station buildings on 24th July, 1955, showing the goods shed and awning in good detail. *E.H. Sawford*

A clear view of Ramsey North Station, showing the corn mill, station buildings and yard in 1955. *E.H. Sawford*

RAMSEY NORTH STATION TRACK PLAN

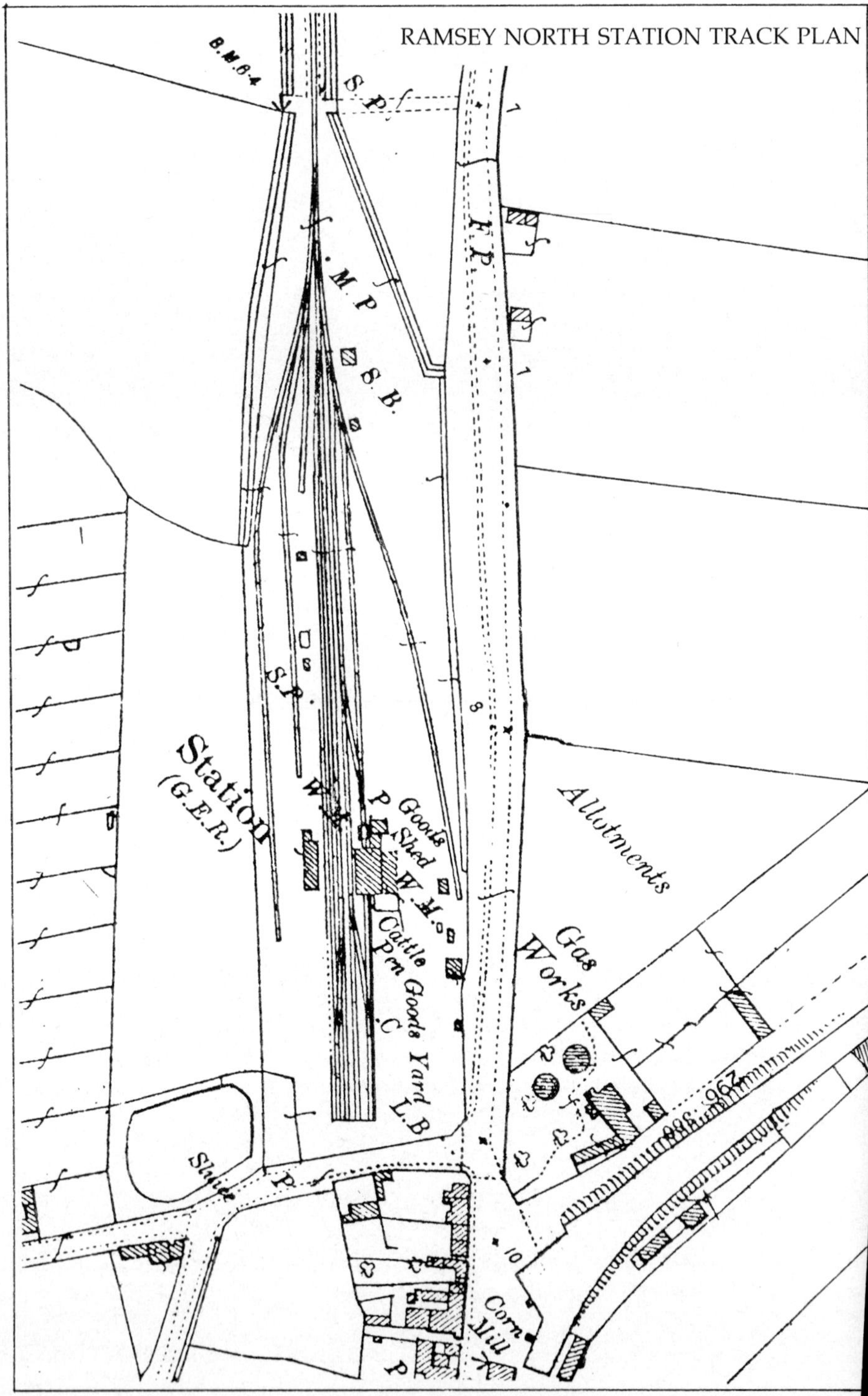

century, the cultivable acreage of this part of the Fens increased considerably. The population of the area was also supplemented noticeably by the large numbers of men brought in to do the work of reclamation, many of whom stayed on and made their homes there. Settlement thus expanded in an unprecedented way, and new hamlets and villages, including that at St Mary's, grew up. By 1861 St Mary's had a population of 1,088, which increased only slowly as the century progressed, but it was a sizeable enough community for the Holme & Ramsey Company to erect a station in the middle of the village, near the local church. This, incidentally, later became a victim of the shifting peat soil, leaning over so dangerously that the spire had to be removed. In Victorian times, of course, even such a modest station was comprehensively staffed, and St Mary's would no doubt have provided employment for several local men, working under the station master, the first of whom would seem to have been a Mr Nathan Jackson. A further sign of the railway's influence on the village was the opening, soon after the line arrived, of the Railway Inn, owned by John Shelton.

As first built, the station had a single platform and a goods loop off the main line with a headshunt at either end, and one other siding running into the yard. Expectations for passenger traffic can never have been very great, but a good deal of agricultural produce and livestock was dealt with, so much so that by 1900 further siding accommodation had been laid into the yard, cattle pens provided, and a substantial signal box (looking too large for such a small station) erected to control movements. The passenger platform, however, always remained very short, and any Ramsey-bound trains much over three coaches (a rare occurrence) would have to stop with the engine standing on the level crossing.

From St Mary's the line continued the dead-straight run it had begun at Long Drove Crossing for another mile or so, over New Fen, until it approached the main road into Ramsey. Here it turned south, parallel with the B1040, passing the Ramsey North fixed distant signal and a nearby sleeper-built platelayers hut, until its arrival at the North station site, terminating a few yards short of Fields Road. Comparison of OS maps from various dates indicates that some changes were made to the station layout in the later years of the century. The 1887 extract, for example, shows an engine shed at the end of a spur between the main running lines and the south siding, but this had disappeared by 1900. In the same period, a signal box was erected at the station throat, and an additional siding laid into the yard behind the main station buildings. These buildings were rather rudimentary, constructed of an apparent mixture of wooden

Another view of Ramsey North showing the corn mill on the extreme left and a more detailed look at the station buildings and goods shed.
Lens of Sutton

The end of the line at Ramsey North, showing the station buildings, yard crane and goods platforms etc. The line was proposed to continue on to St Ives from here but the plan never came into being. *Lens of Sutton*

clapboarding and corrugated iron, and sited some way along the single platform rather than at the end. Opposite was the goods shed, of similar construction, with a canopy on both sides for protection of wagons loading or unloading, and flanked at the south end by cattle pens. A 5-ton crane and a weighbridge office were provided in the yard.

Very little trace now remains of the branch line and its buildings. Having lost its branch-line passenger service, Holme station retained a local stopping-train service until April 1959, when British Railways closed down both remaining intermediate stations between Peterborough and Huntingdon. The station remained in use for freight until the mid-1970s when all buildings were demolished. A new signal box and the lifting barriers are now all that remains, and the only indication that a station once existed is the large expanse of flattened ground alongside the main running lines where HSTs now sweep past unimpeded. One small part of this end of the Holme branch does still exist, however, in that the GN somersault signal which controlled entry to the single line was taken away at closure and utilised on the preserved Nene Valley Railway, near Peterborough, where it once again signals the passage of steam trains.

Both gatehouses are still standing, even though the one at Whittlesey Mere Crossing is now uninhabited and rather dilapidated. At St Mary's a tumble-down shed and bits of platform edging are all that remains of the station; the village hall stands across the trackbed on the opposite side of the road. At Ramsey virtually all traces of the North station have been removed, although the site is clearly recognisable as a large, weed-grown patch of ground between the main road and the grain mill which the railway used to serve. A broken water column stands incongruously among the rubble, a mute reminder of the steam power that in its heyday brought two separate rail systems to this small Fenland town.

Somersham–Ramsey

The Eastern Counties Railway opened its St Ives (Needingworth Junction) to March (South Junction) line on 1st February, 1848, with intermediate stations at Somersham, Chatteris and Wimblington. With the elevation of Somersham to the status of a junction in 1889, extra staff were taken on to cope with the increase in traffic that opening of the Ramsey branch was expected to provide (on the first day of branch-line operations, 16th September, over 1,000 passengers and 45 trains were dealt with at Somersham), and considerable additions were made to the station buildings: new waiting-rooms and

The main station buildings at Somersham Station. This view shows the building, canopy details and ornate ironwork very clearly. *Lens of Sutton*

Somersham Station, south end, showing the two sets of crossing gates close together and the footbridge. *Lens of Sutton*

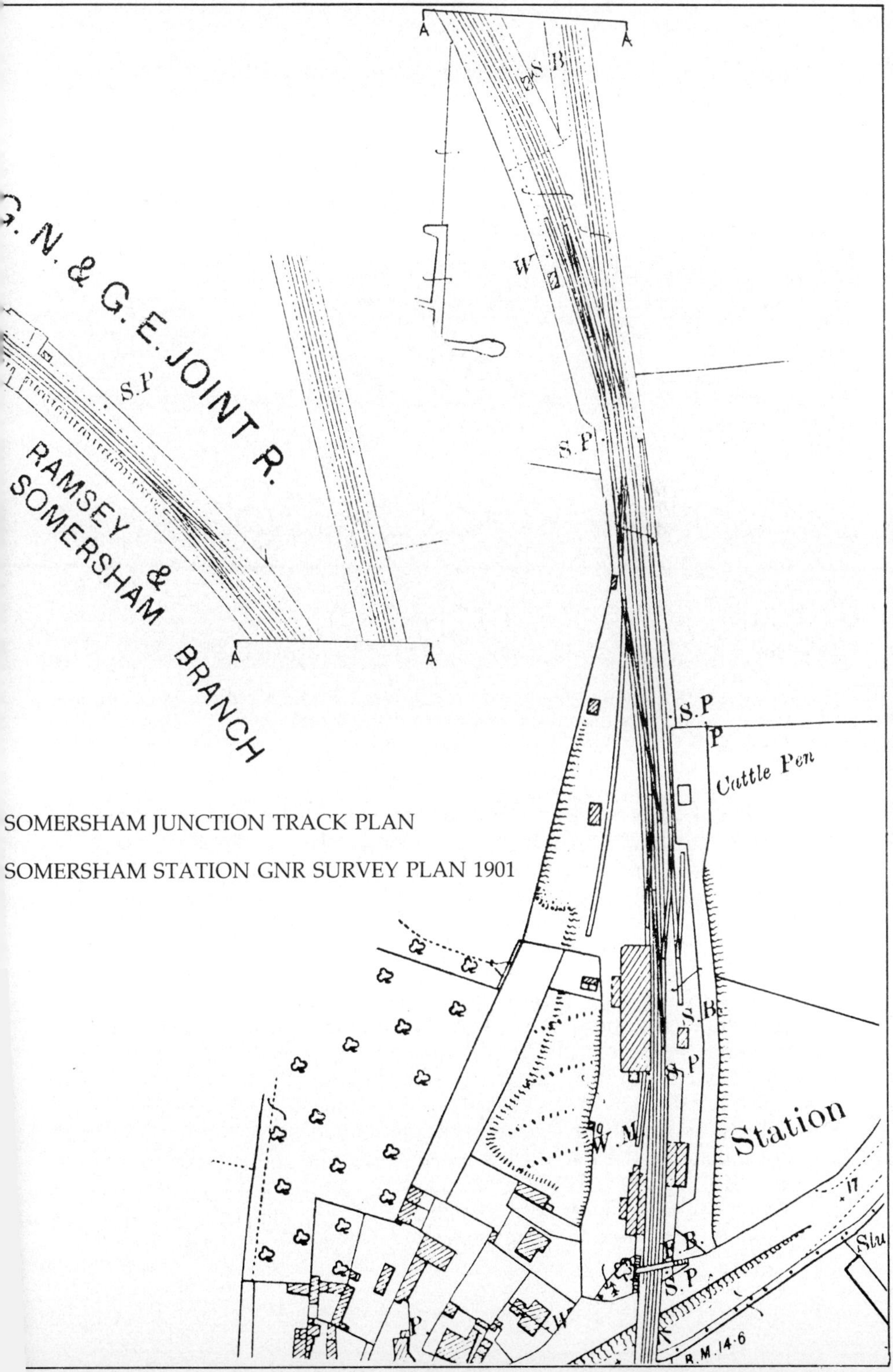

SOMERSHAM JUNCTION TRACK PLAN

SOMERSHAM STATION GNR SURVEY PLAN 1901

Somersham Station, looking towards St Ives with the Chatteris level crossing clearly seen. Note the station architecture and footbridge. *Lens of Sutton*

offices were erected on the down side, and a covered way provided on the up platform, which was extended to take longer trains. The two platforms were connected by a footbridge at the south end of the station, next to the level crossing. There was no separate branch-line platform at Somersham, as there was at Holme, so Ramsey trains worked into and out of the main-line platforms in between other service trains.

The branch line proper began a short distance to the north of Somersham station, the single track curving away to the west and flanked on either side by sidings, which gave the appearance of a three-track running line for some distance. The southerly siding skirted what was known locally as the "Ballast Hole", a deep pit from which, as previously mentioned, gravel had been dug out and used for ballasting the line during construction. At the Somersham end of the siding was a water-tank where engines could replenish their water supply. The junction with the St Ives line was controlled by Somersham Junction signal box, sited on the branch itself. In 1933 this

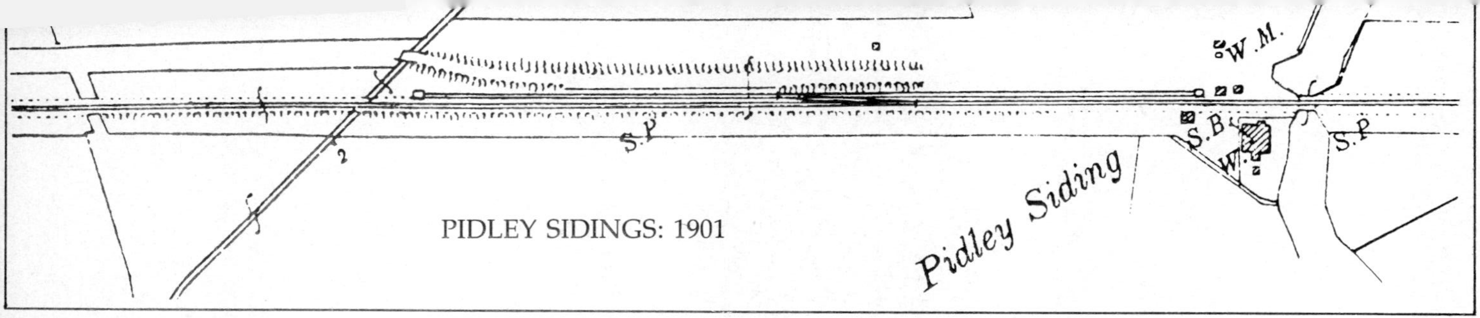

PIDLEY SIDINGS: 1901

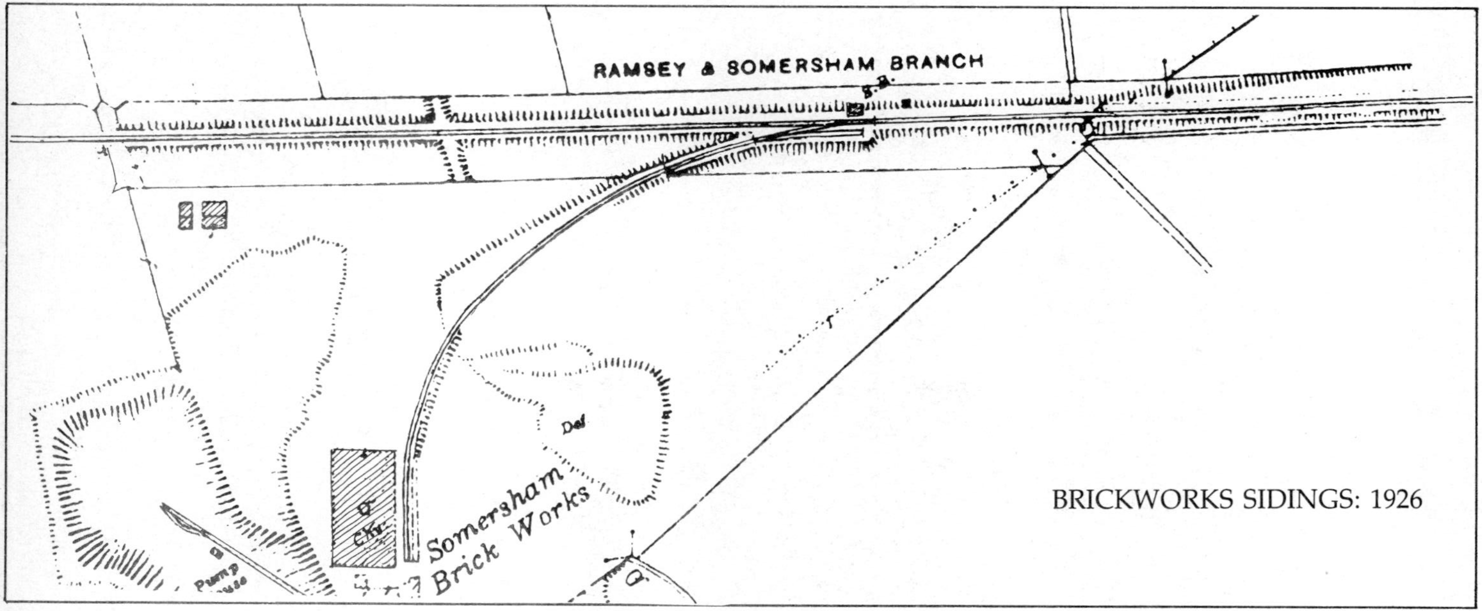

BRICKWORKS SIDINGS: 1926

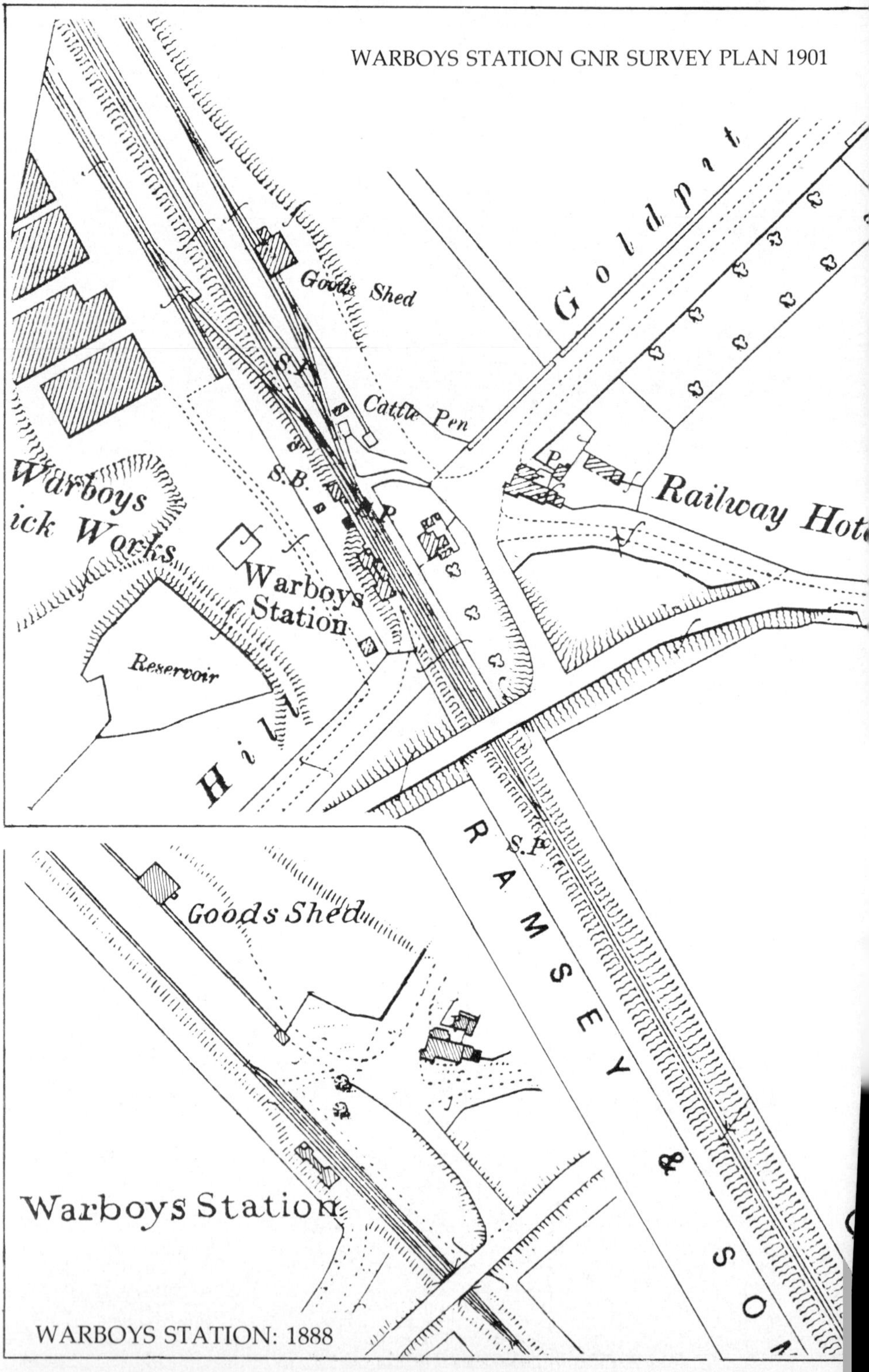

WARBOYS STATION GNR SURVEY PLAN 1901

WARBOYS STATION: 1888

Warboys Station, looking towards Ramsey (the terminus of the Somersham Branch) after the closure of the whole branch to Ramsey. *Lens of Sutton*

Warboys station and buildings in January 1961 with the station master's house in the background. *D. Thompson*

box and Somersham Station box were replaced by a single box built mid-way between them, at the north end of the platforms.

Swinging round in a wide arc until it was at right angles to the main line, the Ramsey line then ran under New Line Bridge, a brick overbridge carrying a country lane, and headed out in a more or less straight line across Pidley Fen. Immediately beyond the bridge, and on the north side of the track, was the siding serving Somersham Gravel Works, which were in operation during the 1930s and which exploited the same seam of gravel which was used for ballasting the line. A little further on, and on the opposite side of the track, another single siding, with a short headshunt, led to Somersham Brickworks, situated in the middle of fields and accessible only by rail. The siding could only be entered from one direction, facing Somersham, allowing east-bound trains ready access by setting back. Trains delivering empty wagons from the opposite direction, however, either had to propel them from Somersham or proceed to Warboys, run round to get the engine in the right position, and then return down the branch to the siding. The 1901 OS map shows a small signal box at the siding exit; this is likely to have been no more than a simple ground-frame worked by train crews.

Pidley Siding, about a mile further on, was located at the side of a very minor road that led from Pidley village out into the Fen itself, and was laid down when the branch line was built as a loading point for the area's farm produce. Like the sidings at Somersham Brickworks and Gravel Works, Pidley Siding (*see plan on page* 67) was accessible only from one direction (the entry controlled, once again, by ground-frame) and was flanked by a loading bank to enable farm carts to load directly into railway wagons. There was also a small weighbridge office next to the level crossing over the road.

On the approach to Warboys, the line crossed the A141 road at Warboys Heath, where the set of gates was in the care of a crossing-keeper (at one time a one-legged gentleman, who must have been pleased that traffic on the branch was relatively light!) who lived in a rather ornate little cottage nearby. From here, the route entered a cutting, passed under a three-arched road bridge, and, four and a half miles from Somersham, arrived at Warboys station, the only intermediate station on the line. The single track diverged into a loop here, with an up and down platform, and a small yard to the north of the line containing a brick-built goods shed and cattle pens. Station movements were controlled by a signal box at the end of the main platform, at the point where a second siding, laid down in 1893, curved round into the brickworks yard, under the shadow of the three tall brickyard chimneys. Behind the station, conveniently

A view of the track work at Ramsey East Station on 24th July, 1955, with the tall chimney (in the background) belonging to the London Brick Company works at Warboys. *E.H. Sawford*

Ramsey East with its weed-grown track in April 1957, showing the grounded box van (used as storage) and a line of goods open wagons on the run-round loop. *H.C. Casserley*

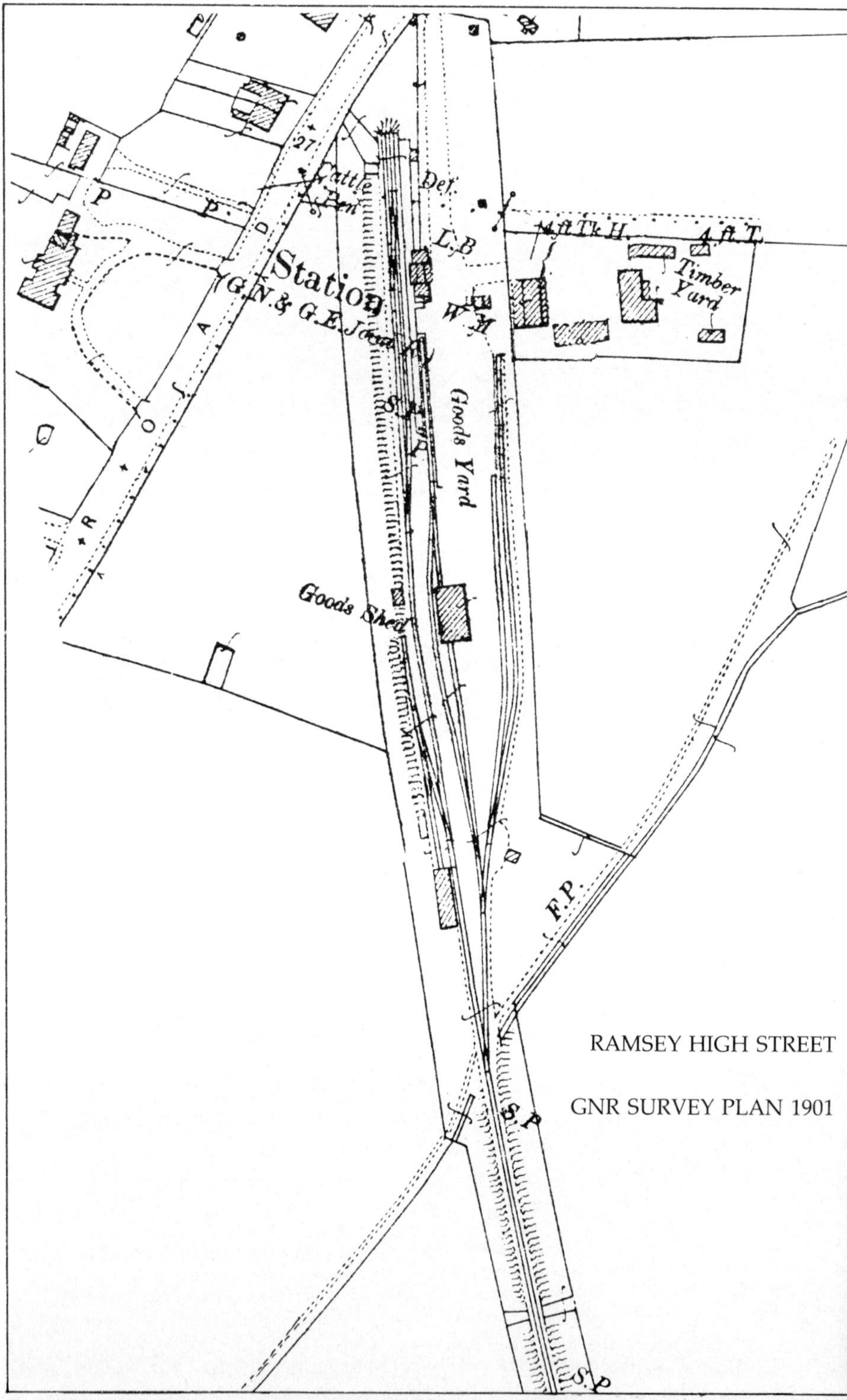

RAMSEY HIGH STREET

GNR SURVEY PLAN 1901

Ramsey East Station, looking towards yard entrance in April 1957.
H.C. Casserley

situated just across the road, was the Railway Hotel, opened at the same time as the railway.

The remainder of the route was virtually straight and level, across the inelegantly-named Bury Lug Fen, with no features of interest except for a few farm crossings, until the line entered the outskirts of Ramsey where it was carried by a two-arch bridge over a small stream and terminated alongside the Bury Road. In its early days, well before Nationalisation designated Ramsey's two stations "North" and "East", the GE station was referred to as Ramsey (High Street), perhaps thereby drawing attention to the fact that it was rather more centrally located than its rival. Although an early newspaper account had referred to the station's "imposing frontage", facilities for passengers were, in fact, on a very modest scale, with waiting-rooms and offices housed in a squat, one-storey building located on the single platform. The yard, on the east side of the station, contained three sidings, with a loop around the brick-built goods shed, while on the other side of the main line was another siding and headshunt leading to the engine shed, with a coal stage and sand bin alongside. On top of the engine shed was a water-tank, which was kept topped up by a steam pump situated some distance away and worked, when necessary, by a steam supply from any handy locomotive. Being at the far end of the station site, the shed was a rather isolated and lonely place, especially at night, when the solitary engine cleaner, preparing the engine for the next day's duties, would hear only the snuffling of cattle in nearby fields and the creaks and groans of the locomotive as steam pressure built up in its boiler. Sometimes the local policeman would call in for a chat to relieve the monotony of his equally solitary beat. All this, of course, ended with the closure of the shed when passenger services were withdrawn.

Somersham station remained open for some years after the Ramsey branch had finally closed, but in April 1966 goods services were withdrawn from the St Ives–March line, followed quickly (in March 1967) by complete closure and removal of much of the track. Some of the station buildings, such as the handsome signal box, were soon demolished, and vandals left their mark on the platform accommodation, actually setting fire to one of the wooden waiting rooms. The fire brigade managed to contain the blaze, however, and preservation was completed some time later when both sets of buildings were taken away to Buckinghamshire where they still remain, restored and in private ownership.

Warboys station is still recognisable, although a new road formation has been laid across part of the platforms and trackbed. The brick overbridge, its centre arch thickly encrusted with soot, still rears above encroaching brambles, and the former Railway Hotel, now a private house, has survived nearby. The London Brick Company works remain in operation, making building blocks, flooring blocks and land drains; in 1975 the bones of an icthyosaur, a prehistoric dolphin-like creature, were uncovered during clay excavation. At the entrance to the station approach road stands what used to be the station master's house, and the goods shed and weighbridge office can still be seen among the piles of bricks in the yard.

At Ramsey, most of the station site has been re-developed as a small industrial estate, and a series of warehouses and factory units now stands along what was the trackbed; however, incorporated into one of these units, and still used for storage, is the old goods shed. Further out from the station, local golfers now drive golf-balls where trains used to run; the former railway bridge over the stream has also been incorporated into the course, and now carries no heavier traffic than golf trolleys.

Appendix 1

Locomotives used on Somersham branch 1960–64

(acknowledgements to Neil Kimpton)

Class J17	0–6–0	65521/28/33/41/47/51/54/55/56/64/70/76/78/81/82/86
Class J15	0–6–0	65462
Class J19	0–6–0	64673
Class 4MT	2–6–0	43061/84
Class 4F	0–6–0	44529
Diesels		D5667/5635/5582/5581/5580/5578/5569/5599/5619/ 5621/5634/5629/5636/5662/5670/5696/5698/5804

Appendix 2

The Scene Today

Ramsey East goods shed in 1984. *Author's Collection*

Warboys station master's house in 1984. *Author's Collection*

Whittlesey Mere gatehouse in 1984. *Author's Collection*